Realise Your Inner Potential

What a man visualises, so he becomes.

Dr. George King

Realise Your Inner Potential

A Spiritual Handbook for a New Age

George King and Richard Lawrence

aetheriuspress

To Cheryl,

With best wishes,

Richard Lawrence

ॐ▲ **aetherius**press

757 Fulham Road
London SW6 5UU

The innerpotential website address is: *www.innerpotential.org*

First edition 1998
Second edition 2004

© 1998 & 2004 Aetherius Press

Richard Lawrence asserts the moral right to be identified as an author of this book.

A catalogue record for this book is available from The British Library.

ISBN No. 0-947550-03-8

Printed in Great Britain by
St. Edmundsbury Press Ltd, Bury St. Edmunds, Suffolk

Cover and book design by Steve Gibson
Illustrations by Alyson Lawrence and Rodney Crosby

Contents

Contents – continued

Index of Exercises

Mind Power Exercises

Psychic Development Exercises

One Energy Exercises

Spiritual Powers Exercises

Acknowledgments

All profits from this book will go to The Aetherius Society, a registered non-profit organisation, for the promotion of spiritual advancement throughout the world. Neither author, nor any other individual who assisted in its writing, preparation or design, has received or will receive any financial remuneration.

Our thanks go to Brian Keneipp, Rodney Crosby, Alyson Lawrence, Nikki Perrott, John Holder, Lesley Young, Alan Moseley, Steve Gibson, Vivien Gibson, Clive Shields, Lynda Shields, Mervyn Smith, Astrid Marie Norlen, David Trimble, Bipin L. Patel and Elaine Gealer for their invaluable assistance in producing this book.

Special thanks go to Steve Gibson and Mark Bennett for their outstanding work on the second edition of this book.

Dr. George King, in ceremonial robes, prior to giving a personal initiation to some of his students. He designed this book as an initiation into some highly mystical practices, for people who would not have the opportunity to receive them from him personally.

Preface

Mankind is on the verge of a great change.

How this change manifests depends on what you and others do. One way or another it will be a time of great upheaval, yet it will also be a time of great opportunity. Because of this change and the opportunity it brings, I have decided to publish the priceless information contained within this book, some of which you will not be able to obtain from any other source.

Until recently there was a cloak of secrecy over spiritual development techniques. The mystery schools have taught them for countless centuries, but they have not been prepared to open up and teach them in an understandable manner to the ordinary person. The policy in the past was that a student had to earn his way into one of the mystery schools, which was very difficult to do. Certain very stringent initiations had to be attained successfully before you could hope to even enter the highest mystery schools, which were located in ancient Egypt, China, Peru, India, Tibet and other parts of the world, let alone receive their powerful teachings.

I am now offering you safe and proven methods of spiritual development which could not have been obtained so easily in the past—and some of them not at all. By performing these mystic exercises wholeheartedly, you will be playing your part in making the coming change successful, both for yourself and for the world as a whole.

There is one way to advance, and only one

If you go fishing successfully you can feed a person for a day.

If you teach them to fish successfully, you can feed them for life.

way. That is to not only evolve yourself, but also do everything in your power to help others evolve themselves.

You cannot do one without the other.

That is why mankind is in the classroom called Earth. Now, as the great change draws near, the need for evolution increases, both on a global and an individual level.

I am releasing to you in this workbook powerful spiritual exercises formerly kept secret by the ancients, as well as new practices given by higher sources specifically for open-minded students in the new millennium. As in all transitional periods, the actions taken just before the change can be the most important you make. You have reached a stage of awareness to be interested in more than just the sea of materialism flowing all around you. You have arrived at the most important time in your evolution—a time of unprecedented opportunity, as well as responsibility.

It is God's Law that time spent doing spiritual practices is never wasted. You are taking essential steps on the path to your own enlightenment, which will pay dividends now and most definitely in the future. Remember, the ancient Chinese sage Lao Zi (Lao Tzu) taught that a journey of a thousand miles begins with a single step.

The only reason—and there are not two—I have spent thousands of hours writing and tape recording the information which forms the basis of this book, is to share this precious knowledge with you. I know from personal experience what it will mean to you if you act on the information contained here, and how you, in turn, will be of much greater spiritual benefit to all you come into contact with in the future if you do so.

From the age of 10 years old, I have been giving spiritual healing to others. It just came naturally to me. As I developed my spiritual abilities, often doing advanced yoga practices for eight to ten hours a day, I had many amazing experiences. I remember one occasion when I physically levitated from the floor in my apartment while I was sending out powerful healing prayers. On another occasion I was able to prevent a storm from flooding London, using a highly complex mystic ritual. I mastered all the basic psychic abilities, such as fully conscious astral projection, advanced mediumship and clairvoyance.

But all these experiences pale in comparison to healing the planet, which has been my mission for over 40 years.

If you go fishing successfully you can feed a person for a day. If you teach them to fish successfully, you can feed them for life. Teaching the techniques I have learned from ancient yoga and developed through my own meditations, enables you to develop as I have done. You too can master the basic spiritual abilities. You too can perform miraculous healing. And my dream is that one day you too will help to heal the planet as a whole. You will then know, as I have often taught, that:

Miracles are not performed by God for man, but by man for God.

I am giving you the practices in this book for you to use. It is not a book to be read and left on your bookshelf to gather dust. In the last 50 years I have taught thousands of students some of the techniques contained here. It is only those students who have rolled up their sleeves and practised them who have really progressed. I want you to be one of these.

As a Master of Yoga, I know that the path of spiritual development promises many varied experiences. Some are inspiring, uplifting and pleasant; some are testing and difficult. But I also know that when you experience the joy of manifesting your inner potential, of radiating spiritual power to the sick and needy, of realising the oneness and perfection of all things, you will never look back and you will certainly never find anything to compare with it anywhere in the world.

I am entrusting the writing of this book to my long-time close disciple and friend, Richard Lawrence, who has discussed in detail all its contents with me. I have personally given permission for the publication of every practice contained in it. I know that if you read, study and, most important, practise what is written here, it will change your life.

You will manifest your inner potential.

Do not be afraid of climbing up the mountain to the temple in the clouds. If you climb slowly and steadily for long enough, you will reach it. Not you might, you will reach it. As you climb higher, you will begin to see more of the temple. As you see more of it, you will appreciate it more, and as your appreciation grows, you will have greater and greater power for the climb. And I promise you that when you reach the temple you will know that every step of your journey was worthwhile.

OM TAT SAT.

Dr. George King
January 23rd, 1997

This book is composed of writings and transcripts of lectures by Dr. George King and the writings of Richard Lawrence. In order to clearly distinguish between the two authors, Dr. King's words are printed in this slightly bolder typeface throughout the book.

By contrast Richard Lawrence's words will appear in this face.

Foreword

In the twilight of his life, Dr. George King decided to write this book with me so that others could benefit from the great spiritual teachings which he practised and which helped him to achieve the higher states. He provided and checked with me all the material I needed for the book in the early months of 1997 and left notarised instructions for it to be published by The Aetherius Society in the event of his demise. A few months later, on July 12th, 1997, he passed from this realm while the book was only half written. It has been my honour to complete it so that many others could share his deep, practical wisdom.

During the 20th century, there have been numerous claimants to the status of master or guru. Some have been from the east, often travelling to the west to spread their teachings. Others have assumed this mantle from one of the western traditions of mystical teaching. Although the term master would suggest a male, it is not limited to men only—nor should it be associated with any particular race or creed. It is universal and denotes that the person has attained the highest spiritual level which can be achieved in our world; that they have literally mastered all the experiences life has to offer and are teaching others to do the same.

Very few claimants truly fit this description. Many spiritual people have demonstrated superb devotion to their chosen path, but could not truthfully be described as masters. It is not for me to name such people—their actions are self-explanatory. At the same time, there have been a few rare individuals, such as Swami Vivekananda and Swami Sivananda, whose wisdom and actions demonstrate their status as true masters. In both cases, the ancient eastern wisdom was demonstrated in their own lives and taught to the world as a whole.

To find a true master has long been the goal of seekers of truth and inner realisation. There has been a concerted attempt by some to decry following a master, the idea being that we should all be our own teachers. Would you try to teach yourself how to drive a car without tuition? Or would you leave a child to discover life's lessons without any guidance or instruction? It would be ridiculous, not to say highly irresponsible, to do so. Of course there is no substitute for personal experience, as some of the most important lessons are learned from the tapestry of life. But to find a successful path to spiritual realisation, you need guidance and teaching, just as surely as you would if you were learning any other complex subject or skill on Earth. And nothing is more important than the inner realisation of truth—or ever will be.

To be taught by an expert is one thing, but to be taught by a Master is quite another. The advice of experts has often proved fallible, whereas a master is one who knows—not one who merely believes or deduces. Therefore you can be absolutely sure that his findings are correct. You can bet on it. I can vouch from personal experience, as can many others, that Dr. King was a true master, but even without these personal testimonies, his life's achievement is a vivid illustration of his calibre.

People have their own idea of what a master is. We can learn a lot from the east. They have tremendous reverence, veneration and respect for their masters. But they also have a tendency to regard them all as being the same. There is an idea that once you reach mastery you are enlightened, god-like, with no problems or suffering. Everything is easy for you. You have all the powers you could want and if you are not exhibiting them, it is because you do not want to. This is a robot-like concept of what a master is. The truth is very different.

Mozart was regarded as arrogant. He used to say quite openly to all who would hear, that he was the greatest genius in music alive at that time in Vienna. This did not make him very popular with court musicians and composers, but he was right! Dr. King, who I believe was a lot greater than Mozart, said many times that he was the greatest medium on Earth. Some people were upset by this, because they had a philosophy that we should all be pretty much the same. But we are not. Many people, for example, study the life of the Master Jesus but focus only on the qualities they choose. They like some more than others: the gentle, compassionate and forgiving aspects tend to be more appealing than the strict, uncompromising side of his nature and the stern admonishments he gave.

If anything, masters have more personality than ordinary people, but they have mastered the ability to control and use it. Dr.

King often said that he was not saintly. He was a very direct person. He always told the truth and he was never reticent in doing so. He was also devastatingly honest with himself. He was a very hard taskmaster of himself and others. He worked long and hard and expected others to do the same. Even as a child he used to work hard—for example, on neighbouring farms. He liked work and he liked to see other people working.

Like all masters, he could demonstrate complete detachment. Allied to this power of detachment was a single-mindedness of purpose. He was able to go on from project to project unceasingly. All his life, he moved from one task or mission to another. He was a perfectionist, whether he was practising an advanced form of meditation, handling a boat or entertaining a guest. He could talk to anybody, anywhere, about almost anything. He had a great sense of humour. If he chose to tell you, as he did sometimes, that he knew the truth about a certain point, then he did, but he was always ready to learn.

He introduced elements into yoga teaching which were not there before. More than any other master, I believe, he demonstrated a sense of urgency and dynamism. "Go towards God now! Remember, even a Saint cannot reclaim a wasted minute," was one of his aphorisms. He was a "now" person. If he decided to do something he wanted to start it now. He lived in the now and moved with the flow of the now. He was strict, but could also be extremely lenient. He put up with things that some masters would not have put up with. He was, in one respect, the most compassionate master I know of, freely giving of knowledge and opportunity. When a master gives knowledge to a student, he or she takes responsibility for giving it. He gave more advanced teachings to ordinary people than any other teacher I know. He was versatile and practical, making a point of doing things like boating, engine maintenance, the decoration of properties, publishing, writing, public speaking, filming and so on. Above all things, he was a master of the Law of Karma and service to others.

I am not saying this to give praise to Dr. King, but to give you confidence in what you are going to read. There are many self-development books available but I do not know of any other which is specifically designed for the modern world and the new millennium and which has been conceived by a genuine master. No other book has the stamp of authority and reliability that this does. Others may be useful or valid but they cannot be as dependable or effective as a spiritual workbook guiding you to manifest your inner potential. It is always best to be guided by someone who has practised what they are teaching you and has demonstrated it in their lives.

When I first discussed this book with Dr. King and one of his leading disciples, Brian Keneipp, we were determined to make it as practical and usable as possible. We want you to get results. That is why we decided that it should be a workbook. I must thank Brian for the invaluable help he gave Dr. King and myself in the conception of this book and many of the ideas contained in it.

There is far too much theory already in the metaphysical movement. Do not take this book on faith. Try it in your own life and I know that it will work for you. It will change your life for the better. But only if you do it. It would be far better to spend 15 minutes a day, every day, performing some of the practices contained in the book, than an hour one day and then nothing for a week. Regular practice will give you definite results. These results will give you confidence to continue and so you will create a pattern of achievement in your personal development.

You may find it helpful to keep a log of your spiritual experiences. These can vary from highly inspiring to disturbing—and everything in between! Although the overall effects of these practices will always be beneficial, you may occasionally have an experience which is not pleasant. If you record these with the same detailed observation as the pleasant, uplifting experiences (which will be most of them), you will develop what the ancient yogis called *vairagya* (dispassion). The experiences themselves will be far from detached—you may feel dynamic and charged up or peaceful and blissful or something more specific—but by writing them down in your own spiritual diary in a detached manner, you will start to develop control over your development. This will be increasingly important the more advanced you become. It will also be a useful reference against which to measure your progress and to refer back, to see how far you have come.

I also recommend that you adopt a regime of physical fitness. You do not need to be super fit, but as you progress, it will help your spiritual practices if you follow a balanced diet and take regular exercise. When you reach the more advanced stages you will need a reasonable level of health to perform some of the higher practices. It is good to get into the habit of watching what you eat and drink and exercising regularly from the start.

The physical aspect is often overstated in mind-body-spirit programs. Of the three aspects, the physical body is the least important, but is still essential and should not be neglected. Hatha Yoga, the yoga of physical *asanas* (postures), was devised as a preparatory practice for the other, greater, yogas. Today it is all too often the "be all and end all" of yoga practice. But put in its right place, this or another system of balanced physical exercise and diet is beneficial mentally and spiritually, as well as physically.

Increasingly, there is disillusionment with political, scientific and religious establishments. They do not have the answers people need to face the challenges of the new millennium. More than ever it is vital to realise that all answers are within ourselves, if only we tap the dormant potential which is there. Politics has its place, but it can only deal with surface effects of world conditions; it cannot reach underlying spiritual causes. Without this there can be no lasting solutions. Although we have advanced scientifically to fantastic new levels, we still have rampant diseases, including many new ones caused by side effects of scientific advances. Science is desperately in need of a spiritual balance. Only with this can it face the problems of pollution, overpopulation and so many others. Traditional religions are struggling to deal with the questions raised by modern science and global communication, and to provide a spiritual dimension to people's lives. They do not have the answers.

The knowledge and information contained in this book does provide the answers. By following this spiritual program, you will knock on the door of your own higher self—which knows. Mystics from every school—eastern, middle eastern and western—have taught that within us all lies divine potential. All knowledge is contained there. By tapping this potential on an individual level, you open the door to this potential on a global level as well. After all, wars exist because of hate. If that were to change to love, no war could exist. Poverty exists because of greed. Remove that and there can be no poverty, because there is enough to go round. How can one person's spirituality change all that? Every person you come into contact with will be affected, whether they realise it or not, by the light you will naturally radiate through you. Sooner or later they too will be attracted by this light and will want to radiate it them-

selves. And so begins a pattern of change which will bring the permanent solutions that politicians, scientists and theologians are failing to find at this critical time in our history.

But first you have to address yourself. Do you have spiritual fulfilment in your life? Have the everyday pursuits of life left a part of you unsatisfied?

If so, this is not a sign that there is something wrong with you—on the contrary, it means there is something very right with you! You have realised, consciously or unconsciously, that there must be something more to life than the drab, routine existence that so many people consider it to be. You are searching for answers and, for whatever reason, you have found this book.

Well, the good news is that your quest has been successful. You were right. There is more to life than most people realise, and I believe, having investigated for 25 years, that nowhere will you find a more complete programme than that contained within this book. It can change your life completely—or as much as you allow it. You are the one who will determine how far you take it.

People look for role models. Some look to celebrities: pop stars, film actors and sports people. Others look to politicians and others to artists. But I have had the opportunity to study and work with a greater role model than any of these. Someone who lived his beliefs for 24 hours a day, for over 50 years. He started practising yoga for eight hours a day after the Second World War, in 1945, at the age of 26. He stuck to it doggedly, at the same time working for a living. Ten years later he had attained the highest known state of consciousness, referred to in the east as *samadhi*. He devoted the rest of his life to using his knowledge and wisdom in service to others and never deviated from this task—not even for a day.

It does not matter what your background is or what led you to this point in your life. Today could be one of your most fortunate days—for you have come into contact with what could prove the key to a realisation you never dreamt possible, providing only that you really practise the initiations revealed in this book.

Richard Lawrence
January 23rd, 1998

The greater danger for most of us is not that our aim is too high and we miss it, but that it is too low and we reach it.

Michelangelo

Introduction
To the Second Edition

As I write this, it is seven years since Dr. George King passed from this earthly plane. More than ever do we need his straightforward, practical approach to the timeless wisdom of the ancient yoga masters. He taught a path to enlightenment combining service to others with personal spiritual development, which is perfectly tailored to our modern world. I believe it is encapsulated in this book, which is why I am so delighted about this second edition.

Since *Realise Your Inner Potential* was published in 1998, it has become the basis for lectures and workshops in the UK, USA, Canada, New Zealand, Australia and Africa. We anticipate it spreading to many other nations in the future. It is heartwarming to receive the many letters, e-mails and comments from those whose lives have been changed by the knowledge and spiritual exercises contained here. I know that you too can find your spiritual key in these pages. And when you do, it will not just affect the time you spend performing these practices, it will change the whole of your life.

Most systems of self-development focus on what you think and feel and tend to ignore what you do. They tend to measure the enlightenment of an individual by the level of their consciousness rather than their actions. This places too much emphasis on one half of the equation and not enough on the other. It is an imbalance which, in Chinese terms, would be described as "the yin without the yang"—a state which inevitably leads to disharmony. This imbalance needs to be rectified and no teacher has done more to achieve this, in my view, than Dr. King. He always emphasised

*I don't know
what your destiny will be,
but one thing I do know:*

*the only ones among you
who will be really happy are
those who have sought
and found how to serve.*

Dr. Albert Schweitzer

serving others as the number one priority in these days, and as the surest path to enlightenment.

It is generally accepted nowadays that negative emotions such as guilt, fear, and grief affect your whole being, that they can lead to ill health and limit your spiritual progress. It is also recognised that the hallmarks of an enlightened person are the joy, peace and positive energy they radiate to others. But, this too has to be seen in the context of what they do. Someone who is only concerned with their own well-being and who spends their time and money exclusively on his or her stress-free, contented lifestyle may radiate a certain degree of joy, peace and positive energy for a while. Paradoxically enough, the more selfish they are, the more at peace they will feel at leading such a life—if they were less selfish they would be spurred by their conscience to do something for others as well as themselves. But this type of contentedness never lasts. Sooner or later, something will come along to disturb it, if only as a karmic reality check to encourage them to look beyond themselves.

On the other hand, a person who has decided to focus their energies on helping those less fortunate than themselves—the abused, the injured, the addicted and the oppressed—will initially experience more stress in his or her life. It is, after all, upsetting when you come into contact with and care about the suffering of others. But, such a person will soon discover something else: a deep, inner peace which no amount of self-centredness could create, for this peace is lasting. To inspire them to help others, they may have experienced some guilt about their own more fortunate lifestyle, they will certainly have felt some discomfort at the plight of others and they usually have to endure some kind of hardship to carry out their mission of mercy. Yet, they are much further down the road to true enlightenment because they have understood its very essence: that we are all one. As the poet John Donne put it: "No man is an island, entire of itself; every man is a piece of the continent, a part of the main."

History is full of people who have made sacrifices and yet through them have found the very thing they are looking for from life. By throwing yourself into a cause for others, your own problems often seem trivial by comparison. The British Charity MIND has shown that getting out of yourself through a creative or altruistic pursuit is one of the best ways to tackle the increasing problem of depression. People who include selfless activities in their life are generally happier than those who don't, for the simple reason that they don't spend so much time thinking about their own problems. They also get the satisfaction of improving the lot of other people in one way or another, which is a type of satisfaction which can never be taken away from you—it brings a lasting, inner feeling of joy.

Mother Teresa (1910-1997) is a good example of this, whatever your views of Catholicism may be. She devoted her life in service to others. She sacrificed material wealth, the possibility of personal emotional relationships and all forms of sensual indulgence. Most people would rule out happiness without any of those things, and yet Mother Teresa was full of joy. She devoted her life to the poor for no other reason than to serve them and by karmic law she experienced abundant happiness. She summed up her life when she said: "The more you have, the more you are occupied, the less you give. But the less you have the more free you are. Poverty for us is a freedom. It is not a mortification, a penance. It is joyful freedom. There is no television here, no this, no that. But we are perfectly happy."

Another humanitarian giant, Albert Schweitzer (1875-1965), devoted much of his life in service to humanity. He was a respected writer on theology, an accomplished organist and an authority on Bach, but he gave all this up to become a medical missionary. He took up the study of medicine not because it interested him as a subject, but because he considered it the most useful skill he could learn to help others. He worked tirelessly throughout his life, building a hospital in French Equatorial Africa in 1913 and later a leper colony there. Through his work—which to many would appear to be the ultimate sacrifice of wealth, family life and the career he originally chose—his Karma brought him lasting happiness. As he once said: "I don't know what your destiny will be, but one thing I do know: the only ones among you who will be really happy are those who have sought and found how to serve."

We all have a unique reason for being here, which is our destiny. We are not all lucky enough to do the exact job we would have chosen in an ideal world. Even those of us who are so fortunate are required to do things that are not our favourite parts of the job. No healer—and I cannot think of a greater calling than this—actually enjoys witnessing pain and suffering. No decent teacher enjoys having to discipline unruly students. And yet both these cases are an integral part of the work and aspects which make it really worthwhile. This book will help you to realise and manifest your destiny as the outer manifestation of your inner potential.

According to mystical writings, we each have within us the same spark of perfection, which is often described as the divine or real self. Along the way, there are numerous lessons, different for each one of us thank goodness, which produce the rich variety of human experience in the world. The quicker we face up to and deal with our own limitations, the sooner we will reach our ultimate goals—just as you cannot solve a problem without facing it first, nor can you tackle and change your own limitations without first acknowledging them, at least to yourself. But never see them as permanent. They are only temporary aberrations obscuring your real, unlimited potential. In Michelangelo's words: "The greater danger for most of us is not that our aim is too high and we miss it, but that it is too low and we reach it."

As the years go by, I become increasingly aware just what a privilege it is to have co-authored books with my Master. This was the last book he worked on, and I was overwhelmed by his spiritual generosity, both in entrusting me with this task and in how much he was willing to give to this project in the final months of his life.

I did not expect him to allow me to publish so much spiritual wealth in one book and make what would once have been secret so freely available. In the modern world, it is no longer necessary to break away from civilisation in order to discover one's inner potential, as the serious student (or *sannyasin*) was encouraged to do when yoga was first taught. It is now a matter of working in the world to help everyone to discover their inner potential and, in the process, to realise your own. The goal now is freedom from ill health, ignorance and every kind of poverty—spiritual, mental and material—for everyone.

You can realise your inner potential in every thought and action throughout your life. If you practise the exercises in this book, they will directly affect every single area of your life for the better. You will express more of your natural ability all the time. And, if you take it far enough, you will develop a new-found spiritual awareness you never dreamed possible. Spiritual development is an adventure—sometimes exciting and challenging, occasionally difficult; sometimes peaceful, joyful, blissful even. But it is always rewarding. There are times when we want to do nothing else, and other times when we want to give it a break. We all have to find our own pace—but whatever that is, it is essential to keep going and to never give up. Results can come quickly or slowly, but they will come providing you continue. We all have unlimited inner potential—it is up to each of us when and how we realise it.

May your spiritual journey be blessed with lasting success.

Richard Lawrence
July 12th, 2004

It is Wisdom that sets a man free. Nothing else.

Dr. George King

The First Initiation
Discovering Universal Knowledge

Mysticism and Secrecy

Throughout the centuries, mystics from all parts of the world have withheld their knowledge, giving it only by secret initiation. This was a deliberate plan to prevent people who were not ready from receiving information which could be misunderstood, or worse, misused. This could potentially harm them and all they came into contact with. Now much of this information is available and this Initiation summarises some of the main points drawn from numerous sources. If studied carefully, this knowledge will bring about a highly beneficial change of consciousness.

As with everything else in life, this plan of secrecy was open to abuse. There were those who withheld knowledge for an entirely different reason—to keep the power for themselves rather than sharing it with others. Even worse, there were those who tried to use the knowledge for their own selfish purposes. This became known as the "left hand path". Mysticism and magical practice in essence are always natural and good. This essence is only lost when people distort the good by unnatural practices. It is not so much a case of two different systems of magic (good and bad), as one system which has been misused and perverted by wicked individuals throughout history. This is so-called "black magic" and should not under any condition be practised. When I

The Sphinx and Great Pyramid were based on mystic knowledge that is now largely lost. The Egyptians turned secrecy into a high art.

refer to magic, I mean positive, natural and good practices which follow sound mystical principles and which are sometimes described as "white magic".

The question of secrecy arose thousands of years ago when the Sanskrit Vedas were written down. These were originally handed down orally—and, for that reason, no one knows exactly how old they really

are. Some say thousands of years, some say tens of thousands and some say more than that. They were reputedly first written down by Srila Vyasadeva, who is believed to have been the literary incarnation of God. This is estimated by some scholars to have happened 5,000 years ago, though this is hotly disputed in Hindu circles. Srila Vyasadeva compiled the Vedas, the Vedanta-Sutras, which are commentaries on the Vedas, and the Srimad Bhagavatam, which is designed as a more assimilable version of those teachings, under the direction of his Master, Narada Muni. He then imparted the Srimad Bhagavatam to his son, Sukadeva Gosvami, who memorised all 18,000 verses—reputedly a common feat in those days. One of the great powers which could be attained by the rishis, who were the fathers of yoga, and their close disciples, was a perfect memory.

So far the knowledge of the Vedas had been kept to the chosen few. One day, Sukadeva Gosvami recited the entire Srimad Bhagavatam from memory to a king, Maharaja Pariksit, who had one week to live, in an assembly of sages at Hastinapura (now Delhi). This was listened to attentively by another sage, Suta Gosvami, who memorised it and repeated it to other sages and so this hitherto secret knowledge spread. It concerned the true spiritual nature of mankind, the origin of the universe and the evolutionary journey of all life. Above all, it was regarded as a key to awakening the spiritual potential of anyone who heard and understood it. Though it can be read and understood today, some mystics believe that its true value lies in the deep awareness that was transmitted at a subtle level by the early sages who imparted it. Indeed, there are those who believe that the Vedas we have access to today are incomplete and only partially accurate.

Mystic knowledge was also kept a well-guarded secret in ancient Egypt. The unwillingness of the early Egyptian priests to share their knowledge with anyone other than a few chosen initiates is legendary. Even today Egyptologists are desperately trying to unravel what exactly went on in the Pyramid Age and before. Estimates of when exactly the civilisation first flourished again vary from thousands to tens of thousands of years. Ancient Greek and Roman writers believed unequivocally that Pythagoras, Plato and Homer all learned from the Egyptians. The Sicilian historian, Diodorus, who lived in the first century BC, said: "The most educated of Greeks have an ambition to visit Egypt to study the laws and principles of a most remarkable nature. Although

this country was closed to strangers, those among the ancients known to have visited Egypt were Orpheus, Homer, Pythagoras and Solon...." Over 300 years later, the Roman philosopher Porphyry wrote: "The kings of Egypt...had made [Egypt] inaccessible to foreigners." There was certainly no proselytising zeal among the Egyptians—on the contrary, they turned secrecy into a high art, making their real beliefs a fascinating source of speculation ever since.

Theories abound about the knowledge of the Egyptian priests who combined mystic knowledge with science. Based in the holy city of Heliopolis (meaning city of the sun), the priesthood was composed of sages and highly trained initiates who were conversant in a number of sciences, including hieroglyphs, the sacred form of writing invented by the Egyptians. This too is wrapped in a coded form of secrecy which generations of scholars have attempted to decipher ever since. Some researchers have tied together their design of the pyramids, their knowledge of astronomy and an interpretation of the hieroglyphs to produce theories of a connection between ancient Egypt and interplanetary travellers.

For every theory you encounter about the Pyramid Age of the ancient Egyptians, you can guarantee that a new theory will shortly be produced. The very fact that there are so many different views about this extraordinary epoch in our history indicates that there was a hidden agenda at work among the priests. Why should this have been? Certainly to protect their knowledge and avoid it becoming distorted. Certainly also because they had an inherent distrust of foreigners and the uninitiated generally. But also because they must have believed, as did so many generations to follow, that this type of knowledge was not necessarily suitable for public dissemination; that it was necessary to prove that you were ready and deserved to receive this information before it could safely be imparted to you.

The Egyptian civilisation did not only influence the Greek and Roman cultures, but was also a major force behind the other great strand of western thought: the Judaeo-Christian legacy. According to the Old Testament, Moses was "learned in all the wisdom of the Egyptians and mighty in words and in deeds." This suggests that he was trained in the ritualistic magic which was prevalent at that time, but given by initiation only. It was regarded as essential that a priest-magician should maintain purity and secrecy at all times. There is a direct continuity between Egyptian magic and Jewish mysticism. According to a Samaritan legend, the Book of Signs, which in the Jewish tradition is called the Book of Adam or the Book of Raziel, was given to Adam before he left Paradise. This knowledge is now believed to be contained in the Kabbalah, the Jewish mystical teaching, much of which was handed down by word of mouth and held in mystery for the use of adepts in magical practice.

King Solomon was famous for the so-called "wisdom of Solomon". Probably many of the great sayings and writings attributed to him were in fact from other sources, and if the biblical account is to be believed, some of his behaviour did not exactly come under the category of wisdom. Nevertheless he has been associated with secret mystical thought and practice, including some masonic rituals still used today. Several 16th-century manuscripts survive under such names as The Clavicle (or Key) of Solomon, The Work of Solomon the Wise and The Key of Solomon the King. According to legend, Solomon was inspired by the teaching of an angel called Raziel, who appeared to him in his sleep and gave him a secret work. This was engraved on the bark of trees and placed in an ivory casket made by his son Roboam, so that it would not be generally accessible. This casket was then placed in a sepulchre and kept in the Temple of Solomon. Much later it was discovered by some Babylonian philosophers when the tomb was being restored. They could not understand it, but a Grecian called Ptolemy was guided by an angel who appeared and helped him to understand its obscure and profound secrets. It was translated from Hebrew into Latin by Rabbi Abognazar (probably Aben Ezra) who transported it with him to the town of Arles in Provence, where it subsequently fell into the hands of the Archbishop of Arles. The Archbishop then translated it into the local language. This illustrates just how esoteric some of this knowledge is and how difficult to come by. It also shows to what lengths people will go in their quest for mystical truth. It was very dangerous information to possess, as Nostradamus, who lived in 16th-century France, discovered. He reputedly destroyed a large number of priceless occult manuscripts out of fear of reprisals by the authorities against himself and his family if they were discovered.

Also connected with the Temple of Solomon were the Essenes. This mystical group traced its lineage back to Zadok, the first high priest in the Temple. The members of the priesthood were allowed to call themselves the sons of Zadok. In time, some of the sons of Zadok broke away from the priesthood, because they considered it had become corrupt and compromising. These became known as the Essenes, a term which derives from the Aramaic word *assaya*, meaning doctor or healer. They formed a monastic community, although some of them lived in the outside world. Their goal was inner self-perfection and they were renowned healers. It is believed by some that Jesus himself was trained as an Essene, but that this was deliberately covered up by the early New Testament writers. The discovery of numerous scrolls in a cave at Qumran in 1947 gave some fascinating glimpses into this sect which has been described as a type of "Christianity before Christ". The Stuttgart town vicar and repetitor at the Tübingen Seminary, August Friedrich Gfrörer, was to say as late as 1831: "The Christian Church developed from the Essene community, whose ideas it continued and without whose regulations its organisation would be inexplicable."

And yet, despite this, very few know of the connection between Jesus and the Essenes, even though both John the Baptist and Saint Peter are said to have been members of the movement. In fact, some say that Jesus' baptism by John the Baptist automatically

Stonehenge as it was in 1853. How the massive stones were transported – some of them over 100 miles – remains a mystery.

made him an Essene. Of course this type of belief was not conducive to the business plan of the early controllers of the Church who systematically set about disassociating themselves from other mystical groups, which they condemned as heretical. The whole mystical aspect of Christianity has been shrouded in secrecy, largely because of the danger of being considered heretical and coming up against the horrific punishments meted out by the Inquisition. Many early Christians, such as the great writer Origen, believed fully in reincarnation, did not regard Jesus as the one and only Son of God but as a great Master and prophet, and believed that God dwelt within every person. Such beliefs were rooted out by the early Church and those who held on to them certainly did not broadcast the fact too widely.

Another group who were practising the tenets of Christianity before Jesus' time were the Druids in the British Isles. Early Christian missionaries sent by the Church from Rome reported back that they had discovered a people in Britain who were already conversant with the message they had come to deliver. Far from finding barbaric hordes, they found a highly cultured, spiritual people, who are often associated nowadays with that ancient, mysterious edifice in Wiltshire—Stonehenge.

Even recently, researchers have revised their opinions on how ancient Stonehenge is. Using advanced radiocarbon dating techniques, some have now concluded that the great stone circles were put up between 2600 BC and 2030 BC. No one really knows yet how the 80 stones were brought, some of them over 100 miles from Pembrokeshire, considering that the bluestones weigh four tons each—almost twice as heavy as the average block size used in the pyramids of Egypt. In addition to this it is believed that the 50-ton sarsen stones were somehow transported from the Marlborough Downs 12 miles away or even further. Was this done by teleportation using superpowers? Was it done by UFOs? As early as 1136 AD, the historian Geoffrey of Monmouth reported that the bluestones came from Ireland where they had been put thousands of years earlier by giants from North Africa. He also attributed some of the later re-erection of the stones to the famous magician Merlin, reporting that the job was done "more easily than you could ever believe" with the help of strange contraptions. Was this just medieval fancy or did he know something which has been wrapped in a code of secrecy ever since, along with so much other mystical information?

Despite this code of secrecy through the ages, some truth has always leaked out. Pliny, the administrator and author who lived in Rome in the first century AD, said: "If you have wounded a man and are sorry for it, you have only to spit on the hand that gave the wound and the pain of the sufferer will cease." This hardly describes a normal medical treatment—it is a mystical ritual in which you take the pain, at a mental level, upon yourself and thereby relieve the person you harmed. It would actually require more at a mental level than just a spit on the hand, but Pliny had obviously seen cases where this was done successfully. A similar type of ritual was referred to many centuries later in England by Sir Francis Bacon who said: "It is constantly received and avouched, that the anointing of the weapon which maketh the wound would heal the wound itself." In this case, the ritual of anointing the weapon would create a mystical link with the wound and bring healing. Considerable mystery surrounds Bacon, who was said to have been the Grand Master of the Rosicrucian Order, an Order which still exists today. He is also believed by many to have secretly written large parts of Shakespeare's plays, in order to convey a metaphysical message to the people, which his high political position prevented him from publicly admitting.

It was dangerous to admit to an interest in magical practices in the Middle Ages, since they were seen as sorcery and witchcraft, regardless of the motive of the practitioner. Even herbalism could be thought of as a wicked practice for which people were condemned. A belief in the mystical power of crystals and gems, which is widely recognised today, was treated as a criminal activity—hence the need for secrecy. For example, history records that Johannes Jodocus Rosa was accused of sorcery at Arnhem in Gelderland (the Netherlands) in 1548 after he used a ring to cure people's illnesses successfully. He was prosecuted by the Chancellor who destroyed his ring in public with an iron hammer and anvil.

Secret mystical societies have flourished in Europe right up to the present day. Frederick the Great of Prussia is known to have been involved in occultism. In 1767 he established the Afrikanischen Bauherren (Order of the Architects of Africa). Its main centre, known as the Constantinople Lodge, was based in Berlin. There hieroglyphics, antiquities and other mysteries were studied. Connected with this Order was an inner Order known as The Knights of Light, whose secrets were published in 1781 in Amsterdam by Gottlieb Ephraim Weisse in *Der Rosenkreutzer in Seiner Blosse*. He wrote that they were "masters in the knowledge of All Nature and her forces…they had also secret sciences known only to the highest among them." Frederick the Great had as his personal librarian a former Benedictine monk known as Dom Antoine Joseph Pernetty, who was versed in occultism. He reputedly believed in the Philosopher's Stone, the Kabbalah, apparitions and superhuman beings. He was also said to be in contact with the legendary Count de Saint Germain, who was renowned as a great master of the mystical sciences. History records that the count lived in the same body for hundreds of years, travelled the world performing magical feats for the betterment of mankind and, among other things, proved the practice of alchemy (the transmutation of base metal into gold).

Certain masonic groups retained the threads of mysticism, though by and large freemasonry has become increasingly concerned with politics, business, socialising and charitable work. In the 18th century, Prussian freemasons claimed a connection with the Carpocratians, a group of Christ's disciples to whom they believed he had taught a secret science. This was said to be passed through the Templars and then via Scotland to the Swedish Rite Freemasons. The Carpocratians believed in reincarnation and the mastery of a mysterious power from the Earth, called Vril. The concept of this power caught on in Europe and at the end of the 19th century a Vril Society was founded in Germany dedicated to its mastery. Originally known as the Luminous Lodge, this Society took many of its ideas from the great Swedish mystic Emmanuel Swedenborg, as well as a group known as the Bavarian Illuminati and the 17th-century Kabbalist and alchemist, Jacob Böhme. A French occultist, Louis Jacolliot (1837-1890), also promoted the concept of Vril as a universal force behind all actions and claimed that during diplomatic visits to India he had met adepts capable of manipulating this power.

In 1890 a Russian-Polish explorer, Ferdinand Ossendowski, purportedly encountered a strange being calling himself the King of the World. This being appeared in the temple of Narabarchi in Outer Mongolia and prophesied a time of destruction, social upheaval and global war in the coming century. After this, he said, superior beings would come from subterranean caverns and live among mankind. Significantly, the Gobi Desert in Mongolia has long been regarded in mystical circles as the area over which a spiritual kingdom known as Shamballa exists on a higher vibratory level. It is presided over by an advanced Being known as the Kumara.

It may surprise you just how much mystical practice has gone on in the west, as well as the east which is more famous for it. This mystical practice has been, for the most part, a well kept secret. But now is the time for truth to be revealed to mankind as a whole.

Truth

The modern physicist Steven Hawking postulates that by understanding the workings of the universe you will know the mind of God. The ancient yogis said the exact reverse—by knowing the mind of God, you would understand the workings of the universe. By understanding how the universe works you must learn more about the mind of God, but it will not necessarily tell you about the will of God which governs that mind. That is why it is absolutely essential that all the barriers are broken down and we return to the oneness between religion, science, metaphysics, philosophy and mysticism, all of which are really only aspects of the selfsame quest for truth.

Truth never changes. It can be expressed in many different ways but it never changes. It is a wonderful fact that there is a fund of knowledge drawn from different historical and geographical cultures, all of which, although they were in many cases completely unaware of each other's beliefs, agree on certain fundamental precepts. This, in itself, indicates the universality and unchangeability of truth.

It is a strange fact that in an age of communication with unprecedented accessibility to

According to a parable by Sri Ramakrishna, if several people were blindfolded and then touched different parts of an elephant, they would have very different ideas about what an elephant was like. In the same way each religion touches on different aspects of God.

all kinds of information through the media and Internet, most people who regard themselves as religious choose to follow the religion of their birth. Even though they are aware that there are several other major religions, they unquestioningly accept the religion they were brought up with. There is no logical reason at all why their religion should be true just because they were born into it. There is no more reason for them to choose, for example, the Christian faith rather than the Muslim, Buddhist, Hindu or any other faith, unless they have carefully examined them all and discovered why their religion is the correct path for them to follow. But very few people bother to make such an investigation. This attitude to the single most important issue facing us all, namely, the purpose of life, the reason why we are here in the first place, and what we are meant to achieve through living, indicates that most people do not care desperately about truth. If they did they would seek to find it.

They generally adopt a far more discriminating attitude to the purchase of a car, a home or the pursuit of a job, than they do to the discovery of truth. They look at the different options available, sometimes taking weeks, months or even years before making a decision about a commercial purchase, but seldom make a rigorous investigation of different approaches to the meaning of life. To find truth you need an uncompromising desire to find it and a complete honesty in your life. As Dr. King said, "Speak truth to find truth." By speaking honestly about your own beliefs you will attract greater knowledge back to yourself.

The great 19th-century Hindu sage Sri Ramakrishna taught a brilliant parable. He likened God to an elephant and said that if you were to blindfold eight boys who had never seen an elephant in their life or knew what one looked like, and took them into the presence of an elephant and allowed each one of them to touch one part of the elephant—one the trunk, one the tail, one a leg and so on—and then asked them individually to describe what they had touched, you would have eight different descriptions of the same elephant. In the same way, said Ramakrishna, the different religions are defining different aspects of God. None of them changes God; they each focus on attributes of Its changeless Self. In this concept of changelessness lies the key to universal knowledge. There are strands, even among apparently contradictory religious faiths, which stem from that same fund of universal knowledge, that same changeless truth. Behind all the religions and spiritual philosophies, there is one universal concept expressed in numerous different ways which echoes through history.

Karma

The most fundamental aspect of this changeless truth running through all religions is the existence of a Divine Law. The Hindus referred to this as the Law of Karma. The Lord Buddha said that to every action there is an equal and opposite reaction. The Bible says, "Whatsoever a man soweth that shall he reap"(St. Paul in Galatians, Chapter 6, Verse 7). Moses spoke about the Laws of God, and the Jewish concept of "an eye for an eye and a tooth for a tooth" uncompromisingly defines this exact Law. The Muslim faith too speaks of a day of judgment when divine justice will be done by Allah.

"Instant karma's going to get you," sang John Lennon; "the mills of God grind slowly but exceedingly small" runs a far more ancient English saying. Which of these is true? Certainly times have changed and karma is being speeded up since that profound English proverb was first coined, but on the other hand, you certainly cannot assume the repercussions of your thoughts and actions, whether for good or bad, will be instantaneous. That entirely depends on a very exact combination of factors within your own individual karmic pattern. It is a question of cause and effect.

In the west we are used to the idea of getting your just desserts, of retribution and reward. The Jewish, Christian and Muslim faiths all speak of some kind of judgement after death, based upon an individual's observance of their religious tenets. But mystics, including mystics from all those three religions, look deeper than this. Oriental religions have stressed going within and personal evolution. Breaking the bonds of karma is seen in the east as eliminating all attachment to materialism. In this new millennium the ideas from both the west and the east are starting to merge. Although karma is an eastern word, in some ways it is very much in tune with western ideas. It is concerned with the essential balance of opposing forces.

The human race is comprised of two forces: male and female. One of the big mistakes many people saw in the feminist movement when it started was the attempt to equate women to men, not just in terms of their importance, but in terms of their characteristics and energy. The male and female forces are two complementary energies. Men and women have equally essential roles, but they are different and this is being increasingly realised. One thing that will become very clear in the new millennium is the true role of women, which has been suppressed through the ages by men. In essence, the creative, rational man, and the preservative, intuitive woman, should combine to produce a perfect balance. This is one of the changes that has been prophesied for this time as a new, more harmonious culture emerges.

But this balance of forces goes beyond human beings throughout the whole of creation. The two forces known as *yin* and *yang* in Chinese philosophy are part of the matrix of energy which pervades all life on this world. The forces of the outer world are unalterably linked to the forces of the inner world. There is an old Chinese saying that "the *yang* having reached its climax, retreats in favour of the *yin.*" *Yin* and *yang* symbolise the two forces: the outgoing active force (*yang*) and the inner contemplative and receptive force (*yin*). In the human brain these are represented by the left and right hemispheres, the former governing the intellectual, rational mind, and the latter governing the creative,

imaginative aspects of mind. Just as two forces pervade the whole of creation balancing one with the other, so within the psyche of the individual these two forces are present.

In culture we can see the operation of the two balancing elements as the subjective and objective approaches. For example, while the vogue in 18th-century Britain, in which scientific luminaries such as Sir Isaac Newton lived, was for objective intellectuality, there was also a rare individual, William Blake, who spoke out, and indeed wrote and painted, against the cold intellectuality which so dominated this wrongly named Age of Enlightenment. Instead he looked to higher, subjective states of consciousness, including clairvoyance, and had many elevated spiritual visions which he sought to convey to the unimpressed public of his day. Such however was his determination and faith in his own personal experiences that he left a great legacy which, many years after his demise, has come to be recognised as a cultural contribution on a par with the scientific rationalists of the time. Now we are seeing science turning to the very thing they had rejected, namely, subjective experience as an essential aspect of the physics of the new millennium.

There was a similar balance of complementary approaches in ancient China in the persons of Lao Zi and Confucius, both living around 500 BC. They represented two very contrasting approaches. Lao Zi was a librarian of immense wisdom and knowledge, who shunned the public limelight and left a wealth of mystical teachings, summarised in the *Dao De Jing (Tao Te Ching)*, which were to become the foundation of the philosophy of Daoism. Confucius, on the other hand, lived very much in the world and the public eye, dealing with the politics and etiquette of the day, as well as mystical thought, being concerned with how to live and with communicating to and through the community as a whole. Lao Zi's first line of the *Dao De Jing* is profound, mystical, with a touch of humour even: "The Dao that can be expressed is not the eternal Dao." In other words, read my works, study what I have to say, but by study alone you will not realise the real essence of this message which goes beyond words and even thoughts. His celebrated saying, "Much speech leads inevitably to silence", applies as much to thought as words. There comes a point when the process of speaking, and indeed thinking, never mind acting, must cease in favour of being, realising and knowing. Confucius, on the other hand, was concerned with the world of

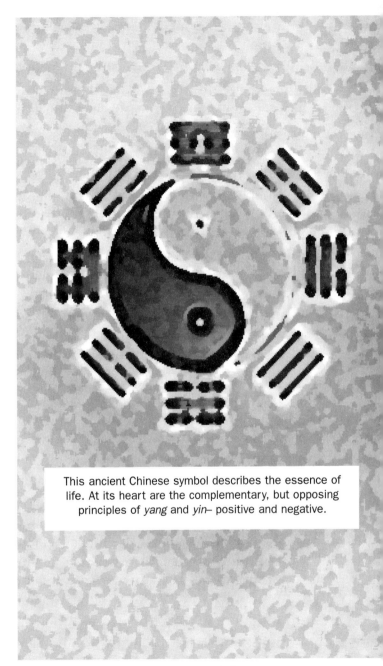

This ancient Chinese symbol describes the essence of life. At its heart are the complementary, but opposing principles of *yang* and *yin*– positive and negative.

action. He was methodical in outlining conduct and behaviour. His brilliant commentaries on the *Yi Jing (I Ching)* are just as much concerned with what people should do as with what they should think or even be. He said: "To study without thinking is futile; to think without studying is dangerous." And more abrasively: "Where a gentleman is ignorant, one would expect him not to offer any opinion."

The same balance of opposing forces can be found in religious teachings. Judaism is concerned with a just and awesome God, Who brought retribution and reward. Christianity introduced the balancing force of love and compassion. Religious philosophy has been dominated by these two essential elements of justice and compassion—both essential aspects of the perfect Law of Karma. Hinduism defines karma exactly as a Law which is unalterable and perfect in its function. The Lord Buddha, who was born into the Hindu faith, introduced a concept of compassion, just as Jesus was to do 500 years later in relation to the Jewish faith. But as vital as compassion is, it is always secondary to the just functioning of an exact Law which, through its workings, brings the evolution of all souls on their journey towards divinity.

The Law of Karma is a natural law. It is a simple principle working through highly complex conditions. By understanding this Law as a natural principle which works automatically and not judgementally, it can be used and turned to the greatest possible advantage for all. It is a law of necessity, bringing you the experiences you need in order to learn and evolve. It is not a system of punishment and reward, but one of teaching and opportunity. The most brilliantly concise description I have heard of karma was given by Dr. King when he said: "Karma is pressure." It is a combination of forces and energies which bring about pressure towards that which is right for your evolution. These forces and energies can be almost abstract and yet they are intricately and perfectly balanced by the Law which is itself divine. Albert Einstein said, "The most incomprehensible thing about the universe is that it is comprehensible." This also applies to the Law of Karma. The universe is governed by this ineffable, unchangeable Law which supersedes all the other laws of matter and nature which scientists are still discovering. When you start to bring your actions, thoughts and energies within this Law, you start to understand its perfection and the way it can work for you in all aspects of your life.

The same law which applies at an individual level (the microcosm) applies at a universal level (the macrocosm). The ancient yogis used to say that if you know a grain of sand then you know all the beaches. What affects an individual part of an organism affects the whole of the organism to some degree. Modern medicine has started to embrace a more holistic approach to the human being, to recognise a relationship between all the organs within the body. The holistic approach rejects the idea of a headache originating in the head necessarily, or a stomach ache purely being caused by the stomach, but sees an interrelating network throughout all the parts of the anatomy of the body having an effect on the whole. Each unit is related to every other unit. This principle applies throughout the universe: what affects the part affects the whole. A metaphysical understanding of life reveals that in the microcosm you can discover and know the macrocosm. Perhaps William Blake understood this at an intuitive level when he uttered the famous wish, "To see the world in a grain of sand". Ultimately all knowledge is contained within us.

The "I Am" Presence

Western philosophy dwells on the famous saying of René Descartes: "I think therefore I am." Yet this statement is at the very least incomplete. Eastern philosophy would say: "I am therefore I think." There is a state of being which transcends even the highest thought, and therefore the eastern approach, preceding western schools of philosophy by many thousands of years, must be the more correct of the two. In all great philosophy there is a paradox. Both these apparently contradictory statements contain aspects of truth but the eastern version is the greater of the two. It has long been known by yoga masters that a divine nature exists within all of us, that it can be contacted, and that at that point, and only at that point, can you realise your true identity. When you say "I Am"' you are describing the highest part of your nature. This is a far greater statement than saying, "I think."

The two most profound influences upon western culture over the last 2,000 years have been ancient Greek culture and the Christian church. I must stress the clear distinction between the Christian church and Christianity. The essence of Christianity pervades the philosophies, behaviour and moral codes of many religions. The church is a specific, organised body with clearly defined dogmas, some of which have unravelled over the centuries as the political influence of church leaders has dwindled.

The great philosophers of ancient Greece laid tremendous store by the intellectual process and the mental potential of the human being. There is, of course, a difference between intellectual curiosity and a soul-deep search for truth. Both have the hallmarks of intellectual investigation, but the motivation is vastly different. This is well illustrated by the story of a student in pursuit of Truth who went to visit a master of yoga in India. The master grabbed the student by the hair and dipped his head into a basin of water and held it there until the student nearly suffocated. He then pulled the student's head out of the basin of water just in time and said, "When you were immersed in that water what did you want most?" Without a moment's hesitation the student replied, "Air, master." The master in turn replied, "When you can say you want truth more than air, then I will teach you. Come back when you are ready." To find the highest truth you need a desperate, uncompromising desire for it.

Post-Pythagorean Greek philosophy emphasised the supreme importance of the human mind rather than the divine self. Plato indicated, though, that there is something even beyond the mind in one of his parables. He likened human existence to people who are chained inside a cave and can see only the reflection of the outside world on the wall of the cave from the shadows created by the sun. One day, one of the inhabitants of the cave breaks free, goes outside and after being temporarily blinded by the sunlight looks around and sees the real world. He then comes back into the cave and shares this experience with those who are still chained inside it. His story sounds so bizarre and far-fetched to them that they think he is absolutely mad and put him to death. This parable illustrates many things, not least the fact that there is a realisation beyond the indirect reflections we gain through the basic thought process. A higher state of enlightenment gives you a more direct perception of truth, even though it can never be fully explained to others. And if people should disbelieve you when you tell them the truth, remember Oscar Wilde's saying: "When people agree with me I always feel that I must be wrong."

The other great strand of thought, the Christian church, also stopped short of teaching the divine potential of all life. In the early years of the church there were those who believed that we all have a divine potential, such as the heretic Arius, and there are still today Christian mystics who teach this. But the dogmatism of orthodoxy established by early ecumenical councils under political control, ruled out this view, along with other early Christian beliefs, including reincarnation. And so the message of the I Am Presence, the divine potential within us all, has not been taught freely in the west, as it was in the east, even though it is possibly the most important single teaching we can be given.

Erwin Schrödinger, who received the 1933 Nobel Prize in Physics for his wave equation which became the heart of modern quantum mechanics, made the following statement: "When a man knows his true self for the first time, something else arises from the depths of his being and takes possession of him. That something is behind the mind; it is infinite, divine, eternal." It is a wonderful thing that a realisation such as this can be achieved not just in the field of religion or philosophy, but through science, the arts and even sport. Almost any belief system can be a stepping stone to the

"When a man knows his true self for the first time, something else arises from the depths of his being and takes possession of him. That something is behind the mind; it is infinite, divine, eternal."

Nobel Prize-winning scientist Erwin Schrödinger

realisation of divinity, but the nearer it is to truth, the further it can take you.

There is an old saying that it is better to believe in the wrong God than no God at all. Of course this is open to misinterpretation and would be hotly disputed by religious fanatics throughout the world. But the essence of it is true. According to yoga philosophy you can never fully know God until you have joined with It in union. In fact, the word *yoga* means union (with God). Until then we only have beliefs. Belief can become your link with reality. As you follow your chosen belief or combination of beliefs, there will come a point when you will have an experience which confirms them. When this takes place you have a realisation which is no longer based upon belief, but upon inner knowledge. You could say that you have then taken a quantum leap. You have, in scientific jargon, actualised the potential of your belief into something real, something you have experienced. If you had not had that belief in the first place it might never have been possible to actualise it.

I was once approached by a society in Great Britain who advocated scepticism, to give them a lecture. They wanted to pick holes in my belief system. They asked me what title I would like to speak on and I selected The Flaws in Scepticism. They did not book me. Scepticism is completely valid of course, if by scepticism you mean discrimination and enquiry. But too often scepticism is a front for cynicism and a purely negative approach. Rationalist and secular societies can fall into the trap of dismissing all supernatural beliefs and paranormal happenings on the basis that they may be untrue, that there could be flaws in them, that they are unproven. But that simply means that you should keep an open mind about them. It is important to remember that everyone, including the members of these societies, has their own belief systems, even if it is a belief in the scientific approach, or even atheism, which is a specific, unproven belief.

Creation

The Druids in ancient Britain taught that matter is the creation of God—without God it cannot exist—and that nature is the action of God through the medium of matter. Perhaps the most fundamental belief any of us can hold is about creation. It is amazing just how close modern science is moving to the most ancient mystical beliefs on Earth about the beginnings of the

Ancient interpretation of THE WORD and major stages of involution and Evolution of Life

Latest and much fuller interpretation of THE WORD and the involution and Evolution of Life

universe. The latest theories on the inflation of the universe or its expansion from nothingness at the beginning of time, parallel very closely to what the Hindu Vedas taught. Cosmologists talk about the "big bang theory", when there was a massive explosion in a potential universe which created the suns, the planets and life as we know it. This has developed into the so-called "grand unified theory" which covers the beginning of creation. Scientists now estimate that this lasted a fraction of a millisecond. Literally in less than a blink of the eye, the universe increases at such a staggering rate as to be incomprehensible to the human brain. It is virtually as good as saying that the universe was created in the "now", which is the mystical concept of the beginning of the universe.

As science moves closer towards mystical thought, it is touching on concepts which it cannot explain except through a leap of consciousness. They defy pure rational explanation and can only be grasped fully at an intuitive or meditative level. For example, according to theoretical physics, the energy of space minus the gravitational attraction of other parts of space must be zero. To put this simply, there must be a perfect balance of forces throughout the universe or there would be a cosmic collapse. Without this, galaxies would split apart from each other, thereby causing a disintegration of the universe. Cosmologists estimate that had the expansion rate of the universe, one second after the big bang, been smaller by one part in a hundred thousand trillion, the universe would have collapsed long ago. An expansion more rapid by one part in a million would have excluded the formation of stars and planets. Even at a purely physical level, this shows the perfection of creation and the obvious fact that a superior mind force, or, as the mystics would say, a Divine Intelligence, was at work. The idea of a cosmic coincidence, which some physicists have postulated, is so improbable, as you can see from the figures I have quoted, that it does not bear serious scrutiny.

Science needs mysticism to look to the big questions about creation and why it took place. The Sufis, the mystical branch of the Muslim faith, summarise the answer to this question by quoting God as saying: "I was a hidden treasure and desired to be known: therefore I created creation in order to be known." Some mystics see creation represented in the ancient symbol of the triangle. It was used by the Indian sages to represent the three aspects of existence, namely, Creation, Preservation and Transmigration.

This transcendental philosophy taught that three forces are necessary throughout manifestation to bring into being that perfect balance through experience which will return all life back to the divine state from which it originally came. The first of these is the act of Creation; the second is the force of Preservation, which is true love energy; and the third is Transmigration through which all life detaches from its material form and returns to a God-like state of non-existence, known in Buddhism as nirvana. As we enter a new millennium, a more complete definition has been given by advanced sources. No longer is the third of these three great forces to be seen as a force of Transmigration, of divorcing from material existence, but rather as the more complete force of Transmutation. Instead of side-stepping, as it were, the physical world, all forms of matter are transmuted back to the source. Matter is seen only as a manifestation of the one all-pervasive energy. Through evolution that energy, in all its myriad forms, will be transmuted until it breaks even the bounds of material form and returns to divinity again.

This is some of the most advanced teaching ever delivered on the purpose and nature of existence. It cannot be understood purely at an intellectual level. It needs to be meditated upon and taken deep into your consciousness so that the higher aspects of mind, the intuition and even the soul can, through deeper levels of awareness, throw light on the inner meanings of this superb all-encompassing philosophy.

It explains the real purpose of life. At some time everybody considers and ponders the true meaning of life. A more evolved soul really cares about discovering this meaning. A less advanced person is content to intellectualise and speculate at a purely academic level without caring in their heart whether or not the answers they find are true and lasting.

It is necessary to turn to ancient Hindu philosophy to find an explanation, which has never been bettered, of this purpose. In the beginning, said these ancients, God performed the out-breathing. Originally there was only potential. From this God chose to bring about manifestation so that all life could gain experience and then return again through the in-breathing back to its divine Source—but with full experience gained. The involution into matter and myriad forms of life was the out-breathing and the evolution back to divinity again, which all life is engaged in, was termed the in-breathing. These two processes were not seen as taking place sequentially in specific periods of time, since time is only a limited dimension of experience, but taking place simultaneously in the now.

As with all great things, it is not an explanation which satisfies the intellect—after all, it only raises a thousand further questions. But it is an explanation which satisfies a deeper part of us, that part which recognises truth. And this recognition will in itself bring greater enlightenment about the true purpose of this out-breathing and in-breathing, namely, to gain experience. Experience on Earth is determined by the choices we make. There is an inherent paradox in the fact that we all have unalterable destinies and yet at the same time we have the freewill to make choices that can alter them irrevocably. Many cannot grapple with this apparent contradiction, and yet if you think about it, it is not really so contradictory.

At any point in time we have a destiny, but it is subject to our freewill and the choices that we make. Those choices alter that destiny in accordance with the Law of Karma. In order to find true freedom, it is necessary to give up our freewill—or to put it more correctly, use our freewill to surrender it to a greater Law, to a greater natural choice made in accordance with the Karmic Law which pervades all life. Those yogis who bricked themselves into caves in the Himalayas for years to meditate, on the face of it took the ultimate step of self-denial and robbed themselves of all freedom; and yet, in fact, they experienced in the caves greater freedom and bliss than the wildest excesses that their freewill could have brought them through material living. By this act of sacrifice freely made, they found a greater freedom, one which was obtained in the only place you can experience anything ultimately, namely, within yourself.

Nowadays it is not advocated that freewill should be used in that way. On the contrary, spiritual aspirants are urged to use their freewill to serve and help others in the world, not to be divorced from it. But nevertheless the principle remains the same: to use your freewill to limit yourself, if necessary, to discipline yourself in certain respects, and through this limitation and discipline, to experience a greater freedom than any other freely made choice could give you. It is extraordinary really that so much attention is paid to the surface physical conditions in which people exist when all experience takes place within them. It is also illogical to concentrate so intensively on just one physical lifetime, when any sensible concept of evolutionary progress would indicate the need for numerous lifetimes to gain the experience required to take us back to God.

Life After Death

The definitive ancient work on life after death is the *Egyptian Book of the Dead*. This is a collection of various compositions inscribed by Egyptians on the walls of tombs, sarcophagi, coffins, papyrus and amulets to help souls in the afterlife. The documents were discovered mainly in Thebes and it is estimated they were copied between 1,600 and 900 BC by scribes for kings, queens, nobility and priests, though they may be much older than that. These documents were in turn copied, in many cases, from other texts—some believed by experts to have originated around 3,000 BC, well before Moses or even Jacob. Of course, even if some of those original documents existed in 3,000 BC, they would themselves have been taken from other documents or an oral tradition which may have gone back many thousands of years before this.

This amazing compilation of Egyptian writings is a hotchpotch of different ideas, prayers and invocations which were translated at the end of the 19th century by Sir E.A. Willis Budge, a former Keeper of the Egyptian and Assyrian Antiquities in the British Museum. As with so many ancient texts, much of it is written in a coded form of symbolism and means little to the modern reader unless he knows the code. The same would apply, for example, to Sir John Woodroffe's treatise, *The Serpent Power*. Based on an ancient Sanskrit text it draws heavily on animal symbolism and other coded references to explain the function of the mysterious psychic force of *kundalini*. Unless you understand these references you are pretty much at sea and get only a vague idea of what the text is really all about. The same would be true of another brilliant text, the ancient Chinese

Yi Jing (I Ching) but for numerous explanatory works, especially those written by Confucius around 500 BC. And many believe there is a secret code in the Hebrew text of the Old Testament.

The most important fact that comes through the *Egyptian Book of the Dead* is that the Egyptians did not just believe in life after death, they knew about it. They refer to the places where the departed go after their passing, and the main intention of many of these writings was to guarantee a smooth passing to the place of their choice. There are constant references to the underworld. Of course, with writings as numerous as these over such a long time span, the concept of the underworld has different meanings in different texts. In some it refers to a lower and most unpleasant place—not as bad as Dante's inferno, but certainly peopled by frightening beings. Some of the texts are imploring the beneficent god Osiris, the Lord of the Dead, to prevent them spending any time in this underworld, but take them straight on to higher places. And you cannot blame them. Comparisons could be drawn between the underworld and the lower astral realms referred to in modern metaphysical writings—and no one in their right mind would choose to live there, unless it was to help those who had to live there.

Ancient Egyptians were steeped in traditions of magic, from which the mystical system, the Kabbalah, is said to be derived. Some of this magic was used for the benefit of others (white magic) and some purely for selfish gain (black magic). Whichever form of magic you use (and it should only be white, because black, as well as harming others, always harms you as well in the end), sooner or later you become aware of the power of the discarnate entities who live on other planes of existence. The Egyptians knew this and they tried to determine their own existence in the afterlife.

Many ancient Egyptians wanted a connection with the physical world from the afterlife which bypassed the process of rebirth. This is an explanation of their obsession with embalming and mummification. They knew through their magic rituals that a person retained a strong connection with physical objects and that this could be used to create a link. The strongest link, strange as it may sound, is with the physical body. Through preserving the body and often other significant objects that were buried with it, they believed they could return after death and wield influence in the physical world. This custom of carefully preserving physical bodies lasted until approximately 640 AD and some believe it was associated with the idea of a physical resurrection—which is similar to certain Christian beliefs. But the early Egyptians had no such ideas. They were magicians. They used mummification to maintain links with the physical world after their demise.

Not all references to the underworld refer to a negative place. Some seem to use the term purely to denote the afterlife and some descriptions are far from unpleasant. The most telling ones of all make the afterlife seem very mundane and this, in my view, gives them a real stamp of authenticity. An example of this is the Papyrus of Nebseni which talks of ploughing, eating and drinking in the afterlife. Far removed from the vague and extremely unconvincing idea put out by the medieval church of heaven being above the clouds with angels, clouds and grapes, this describes a life very similar to that experienced upon Earth. It even names locations there, such as Sekhet-Hetepet, a mighty city also known as the Lady of Winds. This place probably existed at that time on what are now termed the spirit realms, i.e. the realms the soul goes to when the physical body dies. This text gives a definite glimpse of realism about life after death.

Perhaps the most significant writing in the *Egyptian Book of the Dead* appears in the Papyrus of Nu. This describes the seven Arits, or mansions, and names the door-keeper, watcher and herald of each. It is recognised by mystics that there are seven realms of existence (excluding the so-called "hells" or lower asral realms), of which the physical realm is only one. Other extracts show an awareness of the concept of a judgement taking place and there is even reference to the "day of great judgement", which has the ring of Jewish, Christian or Islamic theology about it. They obviously recognised the need to die in the right frame of mind. This may sound an odd idea, but it is one that runs through many cultures and is also the basis of the *Tibetan Book of the Dead* which taught you how to die. If you die with greed, aggression or hate in your mind, you will tend to go to a plane of existence where those emotions thrive, i.e. a lower one. If you are filled with reverence or spirituality, you will tend to go to a higher plane.

The church's idea of heaven and hell instills either incentive or fear, depending upon the person in question, and thereby gains obedience. I have personally hardly met anyone suited to either such a heaven or such a hell—most fall somewhere in between. Hence the greater credibility of Egyptian teaching. Whatever your beliefs about life after death though, the question remains, where exactly are these realms? They are not above the clouds or beneath the ground. They are located in the etheric realms, which is another way of saying, on different levels of frequency or vibration. They are composed of the same universal life force energies as this physical world, but vibrating at a higher or lower rate of frequency depending on your state of consciousness. Heaven is "above" because it is a higher rate of frequency. The hells are vibrating at a lower frequency and are therefore often referred to as being "below" this Earth. Most realms are in between these two extremes and the mental part of our being continues to exist there after death. We go to the realm we deserve to go to. This will either be one of the six realms above the physical plane, or one of the four so-called lower astral realms below it.

Eastern approaches to life after death have been dominated by a belief in reincarnation. Their concern is not so much with the immediate prospect of life after death. They are seeking something beyond this: an amalgamation with divinity. In the meantime they recognise that it will be necessary to have many incarnations in order to achieve this ultimate goal. Life after life will be lived in order to learn the essential lessons which will take the soul into the all-knowing state, known by Buddhists as *nirvana*. One of the more primitive aspects of some eastern philosophies is a belief that the human soul will reincarnate as a member of the animal kingdom: that you will have a life as a human, then a monkey, then a human again, then a snake or whatever the case may be. The interrelationship of humans and animals occurs in Egyptian mythology in a different way, but both are misguided. The doctrine of reincarnation is fundamental to the afterlife question, but it only makes sense as an evolutionary progression. It is illogical to believe that a soul darts around from life to life between the human and animal kingdoms, because of the superiority of the mental and creative potential of human beings (though not necessarily their actual patterns of behaviour).

An interesting statistic, which emerged in the 1990s, is that at least one in four people in the west believe in reincarnation. If you take into account eastern beliefs, this means that reincarnation must be the most widely held belief in the world about life after death. Buddhism emerged from Hinduism, as Christianity and Islam did from Judaism. Buddhist texts refer not only to rebirth, incidentally, but also to different heavenly realms throughout the cosmos, which they call *lokas*. Reincarnation is a fundamental belief which should form the cornerstone of all philosophies. As you progress through the practice of spiritual development, you may reach a stage when you remember one or more past lives, at which time it will no longer be just theory, but extremely helpful knowledge. Even before then you may start to recognise feelings about places and times in history which come from more than just the things you have learned about in this life. A word of warning though: there are some irresponsible teachers who claim to help you discover your past lives easily. This can be dangerous, in that an error can seriously delude people, as I have discovered from individuals who sought my help after being highly disturbed by certain past life seminars.

After death you pass on to another realm depending upon your karmic pattern. The more good you have done, the higher will be this realm. You stay there, continuing to learn and evolve, until the right time comes for you to reincarnate into a situation determined by your own soul. The next physical life will provide you with the experience you need to evolve in your journey back to God.

In this and the following Initiations, I will use extensive passages from Dr. King's lectures and writings. These are printed in a slightly bolder typeface to distinguish them from my commentaries.

This is his analysis of the other realms.

The Other Realms

After death you go to a realm to which intelligences go who are waiting for further instruction. This applies to most people upon Earth today. It does not apply to the enlightened person who can bypass this realm, but it applies to most people. It does not apply either to the evil person, such as a black magician. The average person goes to this realm, where they are cared for by intelligences who have given themselves the task of looking after people who die without any realisation of what is after death. He would stay there for a certain length of time which could be 15 minutes or a year. Every case is judged individually. Then he goes onto another realm, which he deserves to inhabit. It depends on how he has lived his life. If he was a selfish person, for example, he would not go to a very high realm. There he would gain further experience, living much as he has lived upon Earth, though hopefully not in such a selfish fashion. He would live there for a certain length of time—and again, you cannot be dogmatic about how long as time is different on the other realms anyway. Then he would go to the Hall of Self-Judgement, where he would judge himself. Nobody is going to

judge him or condemn him; he will learn to become his own judge and jury. He will then await reincarnation upon Earth. With the help of advisors, he will choose his mother and father and the exact time and environment to come back to in order to give him certain lessons which these advisors, coupled with his own higher consciousness, will predetermine. Then he will live upon Earth, die again, go again to the other realms, and so the cycle will go on and on until he no longer needs to reincarnate upon Earth.

The other realms are more mental than this physical plane. Mental manifestation is easier there than it is here. Here we get an idea and then we have to physically work out that idea. Upon all but the very basic realms you could get an idea and build that idea out of a mind substance, whether it be a temple on the higher realms or, in the case of the lower astral realms, a vicious weapon. In years of psychic research and communication with people who actually live on other realms, I learned that they tend to remember either the very small things, which are unimportant, or the very important things which happened in their life. Memory does exist and it is possible, for instance, for a relative who passed away to recognise their existing relatives on this Earth. When these relatives also pass away they would recognise one another and clearly remember their relationship.

Guides are intelligences who have reached a certain stage—not always a very high stage—and have given themselves the task of looking after individuals and groups of individuals on this Earth. Some of them are quite advanced, but the majority are not anywhere near the yoga adept stage. Generally, communication with guides through a medium, unless this medium has had several lives of strict discipline, is very poor. You may get something like 75 percent of the medium and 25 percent of the guide. A medium who has had 10 or 15 years strict yoga training in this life may get 25 percent medium and 75 percent guide. There have been rare cases when the ratio is 98 percent guide and 2 percent medium. A very evolved guide could not use a medium unless they were themselves very evolved. If a very evolved guide was to try to get his thought impulses through the average brain, such a guide would do physical damage to the medium. In order for any medium to bring a guide through who is a master, that medium would at least have to be an adept.

The help of a guide comes not only while people are living in this life, but also when they go to other realms. The guide can help them through this waiting period. A guide can also introduce any person he wants to help to the schools of learning, which do exist on these realms. Some passage between one realm and another also takes place. The selfish person, for instance, may change when he gets to the spirit world. It is not likely, but it can happen. Instead of remaining one of the selfish masses, he might want to really dedicate his life to helping people. If this happened, he would make a tremendous stride forward, because motive manifests more quickly on these realms than it does upon Earth.

Not all the realms are pleasant. There are lower astral realms, populated by drunkards, drug addicts, murderers, black magicians and so on. You get several layers of involution on these lower regions. There are the really low regions where the worst would go to. They are not like Dante's Inferno, but they are not very pretty places. If you are advanced, you will have had a special initiation in which you have been taken down to the lower realms and have had a vile job to perform, which will be of tremendous value to inhabitants

there. You can do far better work, such as healing and teaching, on the lower realms than you can on the higher realms, because the need for it is so much greater on the lower realms.

While life after death is not the wonderful heaven that some people paint it, it does consist of realms which are very beautiful, and the higher up the scale you go, the more wonderfully beautiful these realms are. More importantly, these realms are very useful inasmuch as people have every conceivable opportunity of advancing and preparing themselves for the next life. It is strange that the further up the ladder you go the longer you tend to stay on the other realms. As above, so below. The more powerful black magicians can stay longer on the lower planes, and the higher white magicians can stay longer on the more subtle planes. It is very difficult to get to the higher realms and that is an understatement. The longer you stay on these subtle planes, the more you learn while you are there. Like the more basic realms, these higher planes too have halls of learning.

On the higher planes, groups work together on different projects. They make certain discoveries which are passed on to the realms beneath them, providing it is safe to do so. If one or two people who had been adepts on this Earth get together where time does not quite mean what it does on this Earth, without the limitations that there are here, they can come up with some pretty fantastic discoveries.

There are four realms lower than this physical plane and six realms higher. They are themselves "physical" at their own level, though vibrating at a different rate of frequency. It is vital to remember always that even though there are higher, more evolved and less limiting realms than this one, none are more important. This is the realm to which all reincarnating souls must return again and again, because only here can full mastery over experience take place. All souls from all the realms come together on this plane in order to serve, advance and realise the essential lessons of life. There is no finer way to do this than to radiate spiritual powers to others.

The Second Initiation
Manifesting Your Mind Power

Mind

The mind is a mystery to even the most skilled neurologists. Despite massive advances in understanding how the brain works, a definitive explanation of exactly what happens when consciousness takes place has never been reached by scientists. It is necessary to turn to yoga and mystical philosophy for a complete answer.

Mind is an all-pervasive energy which is outside of the body. The physical brain is rather like a pin-cushion. When you push a pin into a pin-cushion you make a hole, and the next time you push a pin through that selfsame hole, it is easier than it was the first time. When you—the higher part of yourself—think a particular series of thoughts for the first time, it is a lot more difficult than when you do it for the

second, third and fourth times. You are making a channel through the brain so that mind can enter.

If you regard mind as being an all-pervasive energy, a force or power outside of yourself, your brain as being a receiving set, and yourself as being the controller of this receiving set, then you get a true idea of how the mind works. You can twist certain little knobs in your brain and make your brain receive highly elevated spiritual thoughts. You can twist other knobs and your brain will receive baser thoughts.

The difference between an advanced man and an ordinary man is that one has control of his brain and thinking capacity and the other has not so much control. It is this control that makes the difference.

The main difference between this book and a computer is a result of mind. This book is made up of five types of energy. There are only five major types of energy in this world that we know of. There are five minor types as well, but they are directly connected to the five major types. These five major types of energy come from the sun; the minor types of energy may come from other sources. The major types are what yogis call the *pranas*. The word *prana* means the universal life force.

You might say, how can it come from the sun and be universal? It comes through the sun from a universal supply. The Thing that made the sun made the *pranas*. The *pranas* are not mind, but mind energy; it is mind which moulds the *pranas*. The difference between this book and a computer is that the "mind" of this book holds the *pranas* in a certain way and the "mind" of a computer holds the *pranas* in another way.

Instead of looking at one thing as being an inanimate object and another thing as being an animate object, look at them both as having mind energy but one is in a different vibratory state from the other and at a different stage of evolution from the other.

Three Aspects of Mind

There are three major aspects of mind: the subconscious, conscious and superconscious. Basic psychology has not yet begun to recognise the superconscious except in a very vague way. The metaphysician knows more about the superconscious than he probably does about the subconscious. These three aspects can be summarised as follows: the subconscious governs physical functions—not physical actions; the conscious governs mental and physical actions; the superconscious governs inspiration, intuition and higher mind.

There is no doubt that the subconscious mind is the largest aspect of the mind. The superconscious is physically the smallest part. That part of the brain which attracts the subconscious vibrations is much larger than that part of the brain which attracts the superconscious vibrations. Strangely enough, although the superconscious inspirations, intuitions and so on, are very much higher than the subconscious from an evolutionary point of view, nevertheless the superconscious is handled in ordinary people by a smaller part of the brain.

So what type of physical functions are governed by the subconscious mind? Things like the digestion and disposition of food. The subconscious part of the brain is able to weigh something like $1/10,000^{th}$ part of a gram of vitamin B-1 and send it to a specific type of gland. It is able, when the body is wounded, to call into action an army of microbes and send them through the blood to combat any outside microbes. It is able to form a skin across that wound so that the blood will not leak away, and also to protect the innermost part of the body from outside intrusion by foreign bacteria. The subconscious part of the brain knows far more about physical function than the conscious part of the brain of almost anybody on the Earth. The subconscious mind of a bird knows far more about its own body than the conscious part of the brain of the finest zoologist.

The subconscious mind is a mechanism which operates according to very strict laws and unless interfered with, it will operate in the best possible way in order to build up the body and keep it fit. How can it be interfered with? The metaphysician, when he begins to study, learns probably before anything else that he should not harbour negative thoughts. He begins to discover that when he stops himself harbouring these kind of thoughts, almost immediately he feels better in health, better mentally, more alert and certainly happier. He realises, if he has the right teacher, that these negative thoughts were interfering with the subconscious aspect of his thinking processes.

A person who is optimistic, happy and positive is a person who generally, even if he is ill, recuperates very quickly. The more positive and dynamic you are, the greater the powers of recuperation you have. You can be very ill today and fit tomorrow. The negative type of thinker can be very ill today and very ill this time next year and have exactly the same complaint. They are interfering with their subconscious mind by feeding it negative suggestions. The dynamic and positive person, who will be more optimistic, is building up the subconscious mind by feeding it with positive suggestions.

Nothing works quicker than this— and it really does work! You can prove it to yourself by trying it. Even the thoughts and expressions of another person affect your subconscious for good or bad. Naturally you try not to let them affect your subconscious for bad, but if it is good, you let them affect you. You play the role of discriminator in this case. You know that many times you have been with people who are extremely negative and you have come out and have had to fight with yourself for a time. Other than that you would harbour some of the negative thoughts that they have given you. If you did harbour such negative suggestions, your health would suffer very quickly.

One of the finest brain medicines, which is now fairly well known, is to repeat to yourself firmly for 10 minutes a night before going to sleep, "Day by day in every way I am getting better and better and better and better." You may have heard it a hundred times, but have you tried it? If you do, you will find that it is extremely good. It works because you are sending positive impulses down into the subconscious mind and you are instructing the subconscious mind to get better and better and better and better in every way. And just as the subconscious listens to negative thoughts, so it will also listen to positive thoughts. In fact, it likes listening to positive thoughts best because its main function is that of building up the body.

The subconscious is a very brilliant part of the mind in that it never forgets. I will go further than most teachers have done by saying that the subconscious part of man's thinking processes is that part which remembers all things through all lives. It has a wonderful filing system. It can file away the memory of events, happenings, suggestions and so on, and these can be brought into the conscious mind again through developing the faculty of memory.

The conscious part of the brain has an idea which is erroneous, namely, that it is the master of the castle. The Masters have said in the past that man's worst enemy is the conscious thinking process, commonly called the conscious mind. It is your worst enemy, unless you control it. Then it is not your best friend, but it is a friend, a necessary travelling companion. It, too, is susceptible to all kinds of happenings and suggestions. It is that part of the brain which governs mental and physical actions. Before you move, you think. Even if you move in a split second, you think before you move. The conscious part of the brain sends instructions to the subconscious part of the brain to activate certain nerves, send energy to certain muscles, in order to move your legs so that you can move. The conscious mind is a beneficial aspect of mind providing always that it is controlled. It must be reminded that it is not master of the castle, but a servant therein.

The difference between the advanced person and the ordinary person is that the ordinary person is a conscious individual, whereas the advanced person is a superconscious individual. The ordinary person is governed by impulses sent through the basic senses, through the conscious mind and into the subconscious mind. The advanced man is he who is governed by impulses he attracts through the superconscious, then through the conscious and into the subconscious. The control of the conscious mind also brings about a control of the subconscious. The superconscious part of the mind is that part of the brain which is highly attuned to the highest and most subtle vibrations. Many people do not even realise that they have a superconscious aspect at all. It is latent within all people, and when they begin to learn, it begins to grow. This is the aspect of mankind through which come the highest aspirations, the great intuitions and the elevated inspirations.

Strangely enough, although becoming superconscious man is the goal of all serious students of metaphysics, because

this is adeptship, it is also the dangerous part of the path, especially in the beginning. We all know that people (especially women) should listen to their intuition. If they do not listen to their intuition, they often wish they had. Some men laugh at women's intuition. Do not bother to argue with them; just put it down to their ignorance. But I think we must all admit that when we first started listening to our intuition, we sometimes seemed to be led astray. In this case, it was not the intuition at fault, it was the interpretation of it. The same is true when you first start to develop clairvoyance.

The superconscious impulses are so fine and subtle that you have to concentrate and contemplate on them in the beginning very carefully in order to understand them. It is not the impulses which are wrong—they are completely correct—but the interpretation of them which can be wrong. The superconscious part of the mind can enable the advanced person to receive messages loud and clear from another realm or even, in rare cases, another planet, without any distortion whatsoever. It operates through the higher psychic centres. When the time is right, it will say to the conscious mind, "You will obey me." And when the time is right and it says that, then the conscious and the sub-conscious become tools led by the super-conscious towards some definite, highly elevated spiritual goal.

Concentration and Contemplation

Since the key to all forms of development is control, it is essential to have as a basis the ability to concentrate and still the mind— good powers of concentration before moving to the higher stage of intuitive awareness, known as contemplation. This is an absolute must on the path to inner realisation. Dr. King describes these two fundamental steps, pillars of personal development, in the following way:

Concentration is the result of directed thought. Wherever and whenever thought is directed down a certain channel—good or bad—that attitude of mind is then termed as concentration. Contemplation is something slightly different. It is a state of mind where, number one, the thought is controlled; but, number two, the thought is left open to receive. If you were to concentrate on a flatfish you would examine the fish very thoroughly, even count the fins, scales and so on. If you were to contemplate on

The Exercises

We will now move from the theoretical stage to the far more advanced stage of practice. There is an enormous amount of information around the world, readily accessible in publications, on the broadcasting media and through the internet. But the only way to really learn at a deeper level is through personal experience, which will be gained by doing the exercises.

To make this workbook as user-friendly as possible, all the exercises that it contains appear in panels like this one.

Creating the Right Conditions

It is not feasible to always be in the best possible location, but you should make your surroundings as favourable as possible. Often you will probably be at home. If you have a special room available which you can use purely for spiritual practices, this would be ideal. If not, dedicate a corner of one of your rooms to this purpose, so that you are facing east if possible. This way you will establish an atmosphere through the vibrations you emit that will become more and more conducive to your practices. You may wish to place there holy articles, photographs or books which have a significance to you.

The Buddhists for thousands of years have said that if you would contemplate or concentrate, do so in simple surroundings. Try this as an experiment yourself. Go into an elaborately furnished room with beautiful pictures and clocks and various eastern carvings and so on, and try with your eyes open to really think about something. Then go afterwards to a very plain ordinary furnished room and you will see beyond any doubt that your train of thought is much clearer in the plain ordinary furnished room than it was in the elaborately furnished one, because your mind is far less distracted. Your brain is not moving quickly like lightning from one thing to another.

It would be helpful to keep a set of clothing for your spiritual practices and use it exclusively for this purpose. The style of clothing is up to you, though naturally it should be clean. Some would choose robes, others more conventional dress. A loose-necked shirt is advisable for those practices which involve breathing techniques. Again the special clothing will absorb the vibrations you emit in your practices. You will eventually feel uplifted just by wearing it.

Another aid would be to use incense sticks or aromatic oils, which immediately change an atmosphere, and suitable music, such as new age or contemplative classical pieces. You are not looking for highly rhythmic music and certainly not emotionally charged music for this purpose. It is not so much a question of picking your favourite piece as of picking one that is conducive to spiritual preparation. Your mind should not, after all, be focused on the music but the practice, so very often silence will be the best. But incense and music prior to performing your practices can be very helpful.

You should put from your mind the daily concerns and troubles of life—and equally avoid any physically stimulating thoughts. It is helpful for concentration to keep your eyes closed when doing most practices. By detaching from all extraneous distractions, you will gain a control over your mind which will enable you to give your all to the vital focus of your life, which is your spiritual life.

the same fish you would leave your mind open to learn something about its environment, its physical function, its mental function and so on. The conscious mind is rather like a grasshopper. Immediately we sit down to concentrate on something in silence, our mind hops about hither and thither. If this happens to you, do not think for a moment that you are unique, or that you are a scatterbrain—it happens to everybody who tries it at first. You can get over it.

Some people think they can think about two things at the same time. An ordinary person cannot do this. He can think of one thing, then another thing and then back to the first thing and so on. If I see a flower in front of a tree and I look at the flower and the tree at the same time, what I am doing is seeing the flower, then the tree, then the flower, then the tree and so on. It is happening so quickly that I believe I can concentrate on the flower and the tree at the same time. This is a tremendous dissipation of mental energy. Hence the absolute necessity to control mental energy either on the flower or the tree in order to get the benefit of knowing about the flower or knowing about the tree. There are many exercises which allow you to get some control of your conscious mind. One of the most potent is repetition, or, as some people refer to it, affirmation. A positive, well-balanced affirmation will help you to gain concentration, because while you are affirming something to yourself, silently or out loud, your conscious mind is not thinking so much of other things. Prayer is a type of affirmation. It is good for concentration. If you say a prayer, you are directing your mind down a certain channel. You are not thinking about your next door neighbour's new television set when you are saying a prayer. You are saying some words which mean something to you and which bring about a certain result.

Deep breathing exercises too give you an enhanced ability to concentrate. In fact, the first thing you notice when you do deep breathing exercises is the mental reaction you get. You notice it far quicker than any physical reaction. The mental reaction is almost immediate. The physical reaction—better health, glowing skin, enhanced magnetism—comes later. Contemplation, if you are doing breathing exercises for instance, would make you aware of exactly what is happening to you. Not only would you concentrate on guiding the breath and *prana*, but you would learn what is taking place within you as you do

The Fishing Line Technique

Treat the conscious mind in the same way as a fisherman treats a game fish. When a fisherman casts his fly in order to hook a fish, he throws the fly in the right way as a bait. Immediately the fish bites he lets the line go with the fish on it.

He does not attempt to pull the fish in immediately. If he does, he breaks either his line or his rod. So he allows the fish to go on its merry way, dragging the line with it, until it gets to a certain position and gets tired. Then he begins to pull the line in very slowly.

Regard your conscious mind as the fish, yourself as the fisherman and the link between the two as the fishing line. Immediately you start to concentrate on a certain thing, in will come different thoughts from all around. Do not try to strain yourself, but allow these other thoughts to come in. If they are evil thoughts—and if you are honest with yourself some of them will be—try to block those out. But if they are just grasshopping thoughts, allow them to enter. Allow your conscious mind to just fiddle around for a bit, like the fish that is being hooked.

Let your conscious mind think, like the fish, that it has got away. After some practice you will discover that the conscious mind will turn to you, the fisherman, for guidance, because it will become tired. When it does this, you begin to very gradually but firmly, reel it in. This is one sure method which does work.

Contemplation is that state of consciousness which brings you clairvoyant powers.

It must, because the basis of contemplation is a clairvoyant perception, a kind of spiritual intuition.

it. It is a much deeper state than concentration.

You might choose to concentrate and contemplate on an artistic drawing—one of Turner's skies, for instance. First of all, you concentrate on that particular picture and you notice the blending of the colours, the workmanship and draftsmanship that went into the formulation of Turner's idea of a sunset. In the next stage, contemplation, you would go much deeper and look not only into that picture, but deep into the heart and mind of the artist who had drawn that picture, using the picture as your focal point. Contemplation is that state of consciousness which brings you clairvoyant powers. It must, because the basis of contemplation is a clairvoyant perception, a kind of spiritual intuition. You would not only know about that picture, but you would know about the person who painted it. If you contemplated a bit further, you would not only know about the person who painted it but you would know about the canvas it was painted on, the brushes it was painted with, and even the atomic structure of the pigments of the paint that was used. That is taking contemplation as far as you can take contemplation.

Positive Thinking

The following affirmations will feed your subconscious mind with positive suggestions providing they are done regularly and with as much conviction as possible. They can either be repeated silently or out loud but it is usually easier to concentrate when they are recited aloud. An excellent time to perform these is for 10 minutes just before going to bed at night so that the subconscious can work with them during the sleep state.

Affirmation for Self-Improvement

Every day in every way I am getting better and better and better and better.

This is a tried and tested affirmation which will help you in any area of your life and will improve your overall physical and mental well-being. It is often used to improve health conditions.

Spiritual Affirmation

I am the Divine Presence which is creating perfection throughout my whole life.

This affirmation is based upon the mystical concept that all sentient life has divine potential. By reciting it, you will identify with your real self and reinforce your sense of spiritual confidence. This can be practised hundreds of times a day or as often as possible. Under certain conditions it can lead to an elevated state of consciousness by helping you to become aware of your spiritual nature.

Concentration on a Flame

This exercise can be used to enhance both your concentrative and contemplative powers. First you should practise straightforward concentration by focusing your mind upon the designated object intently and without deviation. Having done this successfully for a while you can then move on to the higher stage of contemplation by allowing vibrations and thought emanations to come to you from the object.

You can choose any object to concentrate upon but a traditional yogic practice would be the flame of a candle. Sit on a hard-backed chair, facing the candle; or if you know one, adopt a suitable yogic asana, and focus, to the exclusion of all else, on this flickering flame. Become aware of your mind and how intently you are able to stay focused on the flame without wavering. You may be shocked to discover how poor your concentration is, but this is a good sign, because it means you are becoming aware of your mental processes.

Concentration and Contemplation on a Text

Another excellent focus would be a spiritual text. Choose a favourite passage from a spiritual work and first of all, read it carefully, line by line, analysing the exact meaning of the words. Concentrate on it without missing a point. When you have fully understood, through your concentration, what is written in this passage of spiritual text, start to contemplate on it by becoming receptive and allowing its inner meanings to unfold within you. Thoughts and feelings will come to you which will throw more light on the inner meaning of the text you have studied. Do not allow your mind to wander off the subject, but do allow other thoughts to amplify its true meaning. You may even start to gain impressions about the source of this text and the author of it.

There are numerous spiritual texts you can use. The following extract is from a work of great philosophy by Dr. George King called *The Nine Freedoms*, which is perfect for advanced contemplation.

Know that within you burns a Flame, an all-knowing Flame, an all-existent Flame, a Flame which is neither here nor there, a Flame which is neither hot nor cold, a Flame which is neither light nor darkness—and yet all of these. A Flame which is not mind— and yet is all-knowing. A Flame which knoweth no limitation—and yet, vaguely, recognises individuality.

As you enhance your practice of contemplation, so will you start naturally to develop your psychic abilities.

Creative Visualisation

The two main tools to harness mind power are positive thinking and creative visualisation. The first of these uses the intellect, which is often associated with the left hand side of the brain. The second, associated with the right hand side of the brain, is the use of the imagination, which is our only creative faculty. With a mind trained in concentration, visualisation and positive thinking can be used as a powerful way to uplift and help others.

Imagination is the explosion of mental forces on a mento-psychic level. It is the result of inspiration, in some cases, and direct intuition in other cases. It is that mental ability which allows mankind to make a picturisation of a particular thing. If you imagine that you are sick in a negative way you will become sick. The subconscious part of your brain will then produce what the conscious mind feeds it. If you imagine that your aches and pains, whatever they might be, are getting better, this strong, definite request is fed to the subconscious, which in turn brings about this thing that you obviously want. If you allow your imagination to control you, you become prone to uncontrolled flights of imaginative fancy and can become mentally sick. If, on the other hand, you control your imagination, you make it a very positive and definite force, which can help you in every way. The man or woman who has an active imagination, providing it is controlled, is the inspired person. This is the great poet, writer, musician, spiritual worker and even the great truck driver or anything else.

Imagination can be strictly controlled and if it is, it becomes a tremendous power which will help you. I bracket the words visualisation and imagination together. Without imagination you cannot visualise anything. Imagination is a direct result of the explosion of mental forces on a mento-psychic level, but you can even take imagination a step further and say that there is a higher aspect of imagination which is the result of an explosion of forces on a psycho-spiritual level. If you are taught to visualise a violet flame, for example, and you do so to the best of your ability, you imagine it is there. It is not there, but you imagine that it is. The first few times it will not be there, even though you feel that it is, depending upon your powers of imagination. If you continue with faith, you will bring around yourself

How to Use the Power of Visualisation

The Aura Cleansing Practice and the Practice of the Presence (see overleaf), used by the Spiritual Hierarchy of Earth for centuries, were given to modern man by the Cosmic Master we know as Aetherius. They are two of the most powerful spiritual exercises using creative visualisation that I have ever come across. Performed regularly and correctly they will change your life for the better.

The Aura Cleansing Practice

The best way to perform this exercise is to stand outdoors with bare feet on the ground, either on the grass, sand or preferably earth. If you cannot do it in such conditions it can still be done anywhere, including in a building wearing shoes, very successfully.

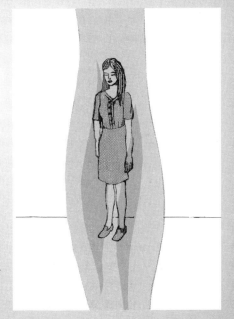

Breathe deeply, slowly and rhythmically for a while until you feel calm and relaxed. Then, gently but firmly visualise a violet-coloured flame coming up from the ground beneath your feet (see illustration). Try to feel this flame, not as a burning sensation but as velvet fingers caressing your body and aura. Draw the power of this violet flame up through your body and aura to a spot about 20 or 30 feet above your head. Imagine it as a mighty flame of cosmic power surging and pulsating through the whole of your structure. By correctly performing this ancient practice you will be cleansed of all impurity on a mental and psychic level. It is also an excellent protective practice.

certain forces which will allow this violet flame not only to exist, but to be brought around yourself.

Take the case of a person who does deep breathing exercises, not so much for physical reasons, but for spiritual reasons, to feed his body and his brain with extra universal life force, so that he can enhance his spiritual work and gain a better understanding. He is told to do a certain practice by his teacher and that when he does so, he will take more of the universal life force into himself when he breathes in and out. But there comes a time when his teacher will tell him, "You have gone a certain way along the path. Now, I do not want you to be satisfied with just the universal life force obtained on the breath. I want you to highly charge the air before you breathe it in, by visualising *prana* coming into the section of air you are going to breathe. In other words, create a magnetic pull; throw out your thoughts and pull the *prana* into yourself mentally—then do your deep breathing physically. The first time or two the student does this, he will not succeed, even though he might feel as though he is succeeding. He might feel that his breath is more charged than ever it was before because of his visualisation of the *prana* out of the atmosphere into himself. But if he goes on doing it, he will create such favourable conditions in his own mental process that he will be able to send out so strong a request for this that it must come into him.

Imagination is the difference between success and failure in all mystic practices, no matter what school they first came from. Never forget that thoughts are things. A spoon is a materialisation of somebody's thought; a headache can be a materialisation of somebody's thought; a great poem can be the materialisation of someone's thought; a cheap, almost unreadable novel is the materialisation of someone's bad thought, and the Bhagavad Gita is the materialisation of somebody's great and most elevated thought. When you begin to use visualisation, everything is enhanced. You are sending out a request; you are creating a set of conditions in such a way that, if it is done strongly enough, those conditions must be brought into being. In your visualisation you think of a certain thing—make it out of mind substance and sooner or later it will be made out of physical substance. The great secret of the opening of the chakras (psychic centres) is the correct use of visualisation.

The Practice of the Presence

Visualise a brilliant white light coming down from above you into your head. Imagine it as a white vibration entering the whole of your head, particularly impregnating the brain. Try to feel the vibration of this energy as it causes the molecules in the cellular structure of your brain to vibrate. Take it down through the shoulders and into the heart centre, which is situated a few inches in front of the centre of the body, at the point where the breast bones meet.

3

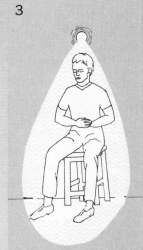

Then, visualise the violet flame coming up from beneath your feet, as you did in the previous exercise, but this time bring this energy into the heart centre with the white light. (See illustration 1)

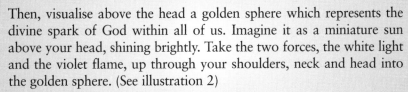

Then, visualise above the head a golden sphere which represents the divine spark of God within all of us. Imagine it as a miniature sun above your head, shining brightly. Take the two forces, the white light and the violet flame, up through your shoulders, neck and head into the golden sphere. (See illustration 2)

Finally, bring down from this golden sphere a golden light or radiance of spirituality, rather like gentle rain, pouring through and around your body and aura, right the way down through your feet and into the ground below. Try to feel the golden rays impregnating your brain, heart and all aspects of your being. (See illustration 3)

This is one of the most spiritual practices you could ever perform. The golden sphere is your divine self. Its radiance is extremely beneficial from a physical, mental, psychic and spiritual point of view. If possible, do this practice every day.

The Mental Hand Practice

There is another law coupled with visualisation. We all have thoughts which we should not have. There is nobody, including myself, who does not have wrong thoughts at times. If you tell me you do not have them, I will have to conclude that you are either incapable of thought or incapable of the truth. Do not let such thoughts go, because you have not created anything for good in this particular case. It is a wrong thought and you have made it. It is on the mental realms, in the air as it were. You have expended a tremendous amount of energy in order to visualise it, even though you probably did not mean to do so. If you let it go it will remain there. When you have the next wrong thought, or the next wrong picturisation suddenly comes into your mind, that too will hang there and so on. Hundreds and hundreds of these wrong mental substances will be hanging on your thought pattern, discolouring it.

What you must try to do is this. When such a thing happens, immediately you become aware of it, try to reach out some invisible mental hand and pull this picturisation back again through the solar plexus centre. The solar plexus centre is not only the area for the great outpouring of energy but also the area for the intake of energy. Pull the wrong thought back quickly into the solar plexus. Imagine that you are reaching out some magnetic hand to pull this imaginative picture out of the ether back into yourself again. Then imagine that you are quickly transmuting it with white light or violet fire. That is the most important aspect of magic. Without it you will never become a good mystic, never mind a really advanced metaphysician. If you imagine that you are doing this, gradually you will make conditions within yourself so good that you will be able to do it instantly. You might be walking along a road and you send out a wrong thought picturisation and you do not know where it comes from. Do not stop to analyse where it comes from, but grab hold of it quickly—back into the solar plexus. Charge it with white light or violet fire and a greater energy will be put into you. The energy that you have expended to put that thought out, consciously or unconsciously, can be drawn back into you and you do not lose anything. More importantly, you will have taken some of the dirty clothes off the line of your future karmic experience.

For example, suddenly a picture might come into your mind of someone you love being knocked down by a car; or a picture comes into your mind of someone you have great regard for falling and slipping down. In fact, sometimes it is so vivid that you think, "Good gracious!"—you actually feel the pain. You may have a picture of yourself slipping in front of a bus or train or something like this. If you are honest with yourself, especially just before you try some visualisation practices, these kind of thoughts do come up. You do not know where they come from. You have never thought anything like that consciously. Your imagination has run a bit astray as it were. Act and act quickly! Reach out the mental hand and imagine that picture back into the solar plexus without concentrating hard on the solar plexus region. Use your imagination in a very creative and positive manner by visualising a white light or violet fire transmuting that picture, burning it up completely and obliterating it. You will get to the stage where you will not have these kinds of negative visualisations. You will begin to control your imagination exactly and you will be able to visualise only the kind of pictures you want to visualise.

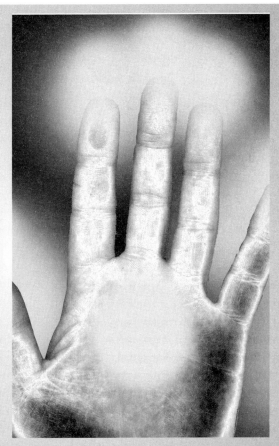

Sleep

We think for 24 hours a day. If you manifest creative, vibrant thoughts of love in your everyday life, you will also manifest this selfsame thought pattern in your sleep state, which is a state of astral projection from the physical body. It is well worth changing our thought pattern to become a creative thinker so that at night time we also become creative thinkers. If anything, that time is probably a time of greater freedom than the waking state. Of the two worlds, I would say the world of sleep is really more a world of wakefulness than this. The next step from sleep is so-called death. After death, the thought pattern, in its mental entirety, leaves the body and it passes on to other realms, where it lives. After death you will not be more dead, or more asleep, but very much more alert than you are at the moment. When you are freed from the grossness of the physical body and you take up residence in a subtle physical body, which is your auric body, you will be far more awake than you are now. You will know greater freedom by far than you do now or, if you deserve it, a greater limitation than you do now. Not only does creative thought help you in this life and in your sleep state, but it also helps you in the next life because you take your thought pattern and your memory pattern with you.

You can change your thought pattern now. You can visualise yourself doing great things now and sooner or later, as true as there is a sun in the sky, you must be given the opportunity to do those very things that you visualise yourself doing.

Memory

There are many systems being taught nowadays to help people to improve their memories for business, passing examinations, learning telephone numbers, making more money and so on. Some of these systems work on a basic level. You can improve your short term memory by, for example, learning 20 numbers which are read to you quickly and then saying them forwards and backwards. These things are not necessarily bad, but they are limited. They may get the short term results people want. They may also help you to exercise your brain, which needs exercise like any other muscle. But they are limited from a metaphysical point of view and in some cases they can be damaging.

Those who teach memory techniques that use negative, bizarre or even violent picturisations in order to remember facts, have no concept of metaphysics. They do not realise there is a Law of Karma which states that to every thought and action there is an equal and opposite reaction. For example, they teach you to remember a name, by visualisation. You might meet somebody called Mrs. Ladywell and you visualise her as a lady who is really well. You superimpose her face on that visualisation and you will

not forget her name. But if you meet somebody called Mr. Sawbone, and you visualise a saw cutting through a bone and you superimpose Mr. Sawbone's face on that visualisation, you will remember his name, but you will have done something else as well. You will have put out a damaging, negative thought about this person. Although some memory techniques are shortcuts, they are not a long term way to really bring out and have at your disposal, in a controlled manner, as and when you want it, the power of your memory.

The subconscious is a wonderful aspect of mind. If you were to listen to some psychoanalysts you would think it was a bad thing, full of hidden fears and unpleasant skeletons in the cupboard. It is not the subconscious mind that is at fault with bad memory; it is the way we have programmed it. The difference between programming the subconscious mind and programming a computer is that the subconscious mind also responds to feeling and imagination. If you have a really positive feeling about something you are much more likely to remember it. You may have a very positive feeling about the Lord Buddha, for example, and think he is a wonderful being who symbolises peace and human attainment. If you do, you are much more likely

*Do not say
"I've forgotten."*

*Instead say
"I am going to remember."*

to remember facts about him. If you think the Himalayas are a really wonderful place and evoke feelings for you, you will remember more about them than your local supermarket, which may not interest you, and so on. Sadly, some people are more interested in their supermarket than the Himalayas, but that is so-called civilisation for you!

The tools of memory are really the same tools as any other aspect of mind development, namely, positive thinking and creative visualisation. The first thing you have to accept is that you can remember. Do not use the words "I can't remember." When someone asks you a question, do not say, "I've forgotten." If it is something you have known in the past, then it is in your subconscious mind, so instead say, "I am going to remember." You can use an affirmation such as, "I am going to improve my memory." If you repeat it for five minutes you will start to feed your subconscious mind with that positive suggestion. The subconscious mind is not against you; it wants to help you. It is only because it has been misused sometimes that it does not apparently work as well as it should do. If you feed the thought into your mind, "I am going to improve my memory", your subconscious will cooperate and gradually your memory will start to improve.

As well as affirmation, self-honesty is an important part of developing a good memory. If you are not emotionally honest with yourself, the subconscious mind will kick back against you. I am not suggesting this from a moral standpoint so much as to enhance your mental faculties by removing any internal subconscious confusion. Whatever else you do, never lie to yourself.

Aristotle, writing about the mind and the memory, stated that in order to think we must be able to speculate with images, and he was so right. The conscious mind needs to use images as well as intellectual knowledge—it needs both. When he taught memory to his students, he used to slap them for no apparent reason. They had done nothing wrong, but in order to make them remember a very important point, he would slap them when he told them that point on the basis that they would remember the slap, which would help them remember the point! The principle of this teaching method was to invoke a feeling, though there are undoubtedly better ways of doing so!

If you perform yoga practices regularly, such as those in this book, you will start to remember incidents from your childhood—and possibly even past lives—if they can help you in this life. A word of warning here though: if you make wrong assumptions about your past lives, you will give yourself the wrong subconscious programming. You may walk around thinking you were somebody you were not. This will confuse your actions in the present. It is better to keep an open mind, if in doubt. To really know who you were, you have to go into a deep state of contemplative meditation, which is above basic psychic awareness. It is always best not to discuss these things with others, because if they are ready to know, they will. There are irresponsible programs being taught to (supposedly) induce past life recall which have caused confusion. As with psychic development, it is best to be cautious and discriminating, especially in the early stages.

Memory is really just a focus of consciousness upon the past. With concentrative memory you can look at language, facts, images, numbers and so on. With contemplative memory you can start to remember impressions, feelings, realisations about people and things that you have learned from the past. The subconscious mind will then be activated in a natural, harmonious way and teach you things you need to know. In a vague way at first, contemplative memory will start to tap into memories from past lives—though not necessarily details, names or places, which may not matter anyway. Contemplative memory will also help you to recall things when you need them, even though you may not have been consciously trying to remember them at that time.

There is an ancient yogic secret that if you know two times then you will know the third. If you know the past and present, for example, then you can know the future. You can know the future that is determined by the past and the present. Equally, if you know the present and future, you can know the past. Advanced memory is related, to some extent, to clairvoyant ability. Dr. King sums up the faculty of memory in the following way:

Everything we have ever learned throughout our past lives is known to the subconscious mind. It is collated quite automatically and is put away in a complex system of filing for when, at some future time, it might be needed. We can all, each and every one of us, transmute the state of mentality called forgetfulness.

If we regard the subconscious as a filing system and if we declare firmly to our conscious self that we have access to this filing system whenever we need it, and if we make some kind of move towards having this access, we can pull out of that filing system memories of past events so that these memories will help us in our present life.

No man and no force can abolish memory.

Franklin D. Roosevelt

One of the first manifestations of superconsciousness is clairvoyance.

Dr. George King

The Third Initiation
Developing Your Psychic Abilities

Psychic Development

As a master of yoga, Dr. King has introduced, in my view, a more complete and balanced approach to psychic development than any other teacher I have come across. Rather than advocating detachment from psychic awareness, as the psychic centres start to unfold their potential, he has taught safe methods to harness and use psychic abilities. At a later stage, when the student is ready to move into the highest stages of superconscious awareness, it will be necessary to reject the basic psychic abilities, but as Dr. King has always pointed out, you cannot reject something you have not first attained. When I first started to develop psychic abilities, I was fortunate enough to receive personal instruction from Dr. King, who gave me the simple but crucial advice: "If you don't use them, you'll lose them." Psychic potential is there for us all to realise and use to help others as well as ourselves. There are many ways of doing this—from healing the sick to giving psychic consultation to those in need; to helping those suffering bereavement and whose departed loved ones are still around them; to generally using your intuition as a guide through life.

One myth is that a so-called "sixth sense" exists. In fact there are five senses, each of which can be extended psychically. Psychic vision is another term for clairvoyance. As well as looking into the future and past, as Dr. King described, it is possible to see psychically the aura of people and places, and to see those who are not physically alive but now live on other realms. Psychic hearing, the other well-known method, is called clairaudience. Through this ability, you can receive messages from those on other realms without the need for any form of trance condition, which can be dangerous, or a practice like the ouija board which should be avoided since it can lead to uncontrolled psychic events. Clairaudience teaches you better than any other method to discriminate between your own inspired thoughts and those impressions received from others which will be received by the clairaudient with the psychic sound of a particular accent or emphasis. If done correctly, it is a precise, controlled practice which you can switch on and off like a tap. It has nothing to do with those who think they are hearing vague voices in their head. If in doubt always turn back to yoga methods for the discipline and control to discriminate correctly between your own imagination and definite psychic experiences.

It is also possible to develop psychic touch through psychometry, which is a wonderful practice explained later in this Initiation. Psychic smell and even psychic taste are also used, though less frequently. They are all methods of registering psychic impressions through using one of the five senses virtually as a meter. You may not get one of the five psychic senses, but just a general feeling, which is known as clairsentience. This too, if developed correctly, can be extremely useful. But of them all, the intuition is the most valuable psychic attribute because it gives you the interpretive ability without which psychic abilities are useless to you. No matter what psychic experiences you have, and we all differ in this respect, your intuition will always be essential.

Psychic development is a matter of finding the key to unlock your own inner potential. Since psychic awareness is a form of feeling, you would be advised to choose those methods which attract you the most. Examples would include psychometry, pendulum dowsing and healing, all of which are taught in this book. Remember, though, that psychic development is only a stepping stone along the way, not a goal in itself. Some of us develop in one way, others in another; but it should lead ultimately to a greater stage of awareness beyond psychic powers.

Clairvoyance

One of the first manifestations of super-consciousness is clairvoyance, which means clear vision. It is brought about by the development of certain psychic centres which causes the transference of sensitivity from the basic senses to their etheric counterparts. If you practise spiritual exercises diligently you will enhance certain basic psychic centres. When the basic centres are opened then you have a greater awareness of the influx and outflow of energy through these centres.

An ordinary person is continually using his basic psychic centres, or allowing them to use him, but he is not aware of their existence. He does not realise that the little floodgates in the subtle auric bodies around him allow energies to enter and leave. As he becomes aware of this very natural process, he starts to develop clairvoyance. From this metaphysical explanation you can see that clairvoyance is not a gift for the few, but something everyone can learn as a stepping stone on the path of advancement.

Some years ago, the general consensus of opinion was that all clairvoyance came through the ability to analyse the interaction and explosion of forces at the christ centre—the psychic centre situated between the physical eyes, sometimes referred to as the third eye. Most clairvoyance is a result of the ability to analyse the interaction and explosive reaction of forces passing through the solar plexus centre. When the solar plexus centre is opened, one has particularly good clairvoyant powers.

Please do not underestimate this centre. Without the solar plexus centre operating as it does, none of you could live—certainly not in this environment, and certainly not in the physical bodies you now inhabit. You are greatly dependent on the flow of forces into the aura and out from the aura through the solar plexus centre. Without this you would have to have entirely different bodies on an entirely different energy system in order to enable life to exist in the robots that you now manipulate through life—the body being a robot driven by mind impulses.

The brain is capable of picking up mind energy and translating this into Japanese, French, English, Sanskrit, etc. It is capable of picking up these very quick, flowing energies, which exist in the "mind sea" around us, and slowing them down so much that we are able to translate them, or part of them, into a relatively slow energy, namely, sound.

Mind itself in free space is capable of velocities up to and exceeding four million times the speed of light. To pick up energies travelling at that velocity and slow them down to about 700 miles per hour (1126 kilometres per hour), is a capability which is built into your brain system and you do it every time you speak. When you translate mind normally, you translate it on a basic time level—you have no translatable time shift. You might know that it will rain because you are capable of feeling barometric pressure on the body. But if you had a translation through a time shift, you could walk into a strange town and say, "Well, it rained here at nine o'clock yesterday or it will rain here at nine o'clock tomorrow."

What have you done? You have become aware of the time shift. You have sent your mind back through time and forward into the future, and you have understood better the sea of mind around you. This is a form of clairvoyance.

Let us not forget that everything which has ever happened and, according to the Masters, everything that will ever happen,

is virtually lodged in the auric envelope of this and every other planet. This is sometimes referred to as the Akashic Records—*akasha* being the Sanskrit word for ether.

This does not mean to say that every little thing is predetermined, because future destiny can be altered; but at any point in time, past and future patterns are lodged in the auras of people, places and even planets in etheric matter. If you walk into any town, for instance, you are able, if you are clairvoyant, to say what happened in the past and you would be correct. You tuned back and picked up the "mind essence" which had the imprint of past events. You could put your mind through another time shift, move it forward to tomorrow, next week, next month, next year or even ten years' time.

This ability to shift the brain through time, either backwards or forwards, comes with the correct balance and development of the psychic centres, without which we have no life, never mind clairvoyant ability.

Psychometry

One of the finest and most balanced methods of psychic development is psychometry.

Psychometry is the psychic faculty of touch.

How does it work? Take, for example, an ordinary watch which is composed of more non-matter than matter. The atoms in that watch are a long way away from one another in comparison with their size. There is more space in that watch than there are atoms of material. This goes for material things in general. It does not matter how dense they appear to be, there are nevertheless more spaces between atoms and these spaces cover a larger area than the atoms themselves. The yogis knew what those spaces were thousands of years ago. They did not need any complicated electronic devices to measure the spaces; they used their psychic faculties. Those spaces are composed of substances which can be woven into any pattern conceivable by man or God, whether that substance be a subtle body, which is invisible but nevertheless quite material, or whether it be a dull metal, such as a watch.

Pervading all matter is that substance or energy we call "mind". So there are atoms of material moving in a certain state, with a certain inner rotation, in an etheric field held together by mind. That is how the Divine Architect created all things. Even a watch has mind. Everything has mind. It would not quite be right to say that this watch has "a mind", but it would be right to say that this watch has "mind". It even has feeling. Some people have cut metal, have tested it after cutting it and have found that it will stand so much pressure before metal fatigue sets in. Then they have cut the same piece of metal but after giving it an anaesthetic. They have discovered that this metal, after being anaesthetised, has less fatigue, can stand greater pressure than the metal did without being given an anaesthetic. Treat a piece of metal or any material object wrongly and fatigue will set in quickly. Treat that material object with great care and fatigue is offset for a longer period of time.

There is no such thing as an inanimate object. It is completely impossible, unless God sees fit to alter His original building plans—and this will not happen because it would contravene the Law upon which all things exist.

If somebody handles that watch, they send into the mind substance, which holds under stress the etheric fields of this watch, a certain emanation or vibration from themselves. It is an electro-pranic discharge. Ether is infinitely variable into any conceivable pattern, and because it is, this electro-pranic discharge, which comes from anyone handling a watch, will tend to impress itself upon the etheric spaces. A psychometrist then takes hold of the watch and, if sensitive enough, can feel through the fingertips, not so much the atomic structure, but the state of mind of this particular article. They can feel the emanations which are radiating from these etheric spaces. The psychometrist can feel, with sufficient practice, any emanations which vibrate in the same basic framework as themselves. You can pick it up, feel it or stroke it and you can feel many things about the handler of the watch. Two hundred years later, a good sensitive could come along and pick up the vibrations of the wearer of the watch, including their childhood and aspects of their life until they ceased wearing the watch, unless it had been attacked too much by weather or other conditions.

When you first start psychometry, you must be prepared to make mistakes, and it is a good idea to test yourself as you go along. This can be done by psychometrising an object which has been worn only by one person, and that person telling you where you are right and where you are wrong. In this way you gradually learn more and more until you come to a stage where you can be accurate.

You are virtually a psychometric machine. When you go into a building, you can feel the radiation given off. It may depress you or, if the building is holy, raise you up to great heights of inspiration. This is another example of the same faculty.

If you develop psychometry keenly so that you can take hold of an article and psychometrise it exactly, you become sensitive to this faculty generally. When you walk into a room, you are more aware of the emanations in that room. If you take psychometry too far and do not control this faculty, you will be picking up radiations from everyone you meet, from every place you go to, and your life can become difficult. The more sensitive you are the more difficult it will become. So, like all other psychic faculties, it has to be strictly controlled.

You should be able to turn it on and off at will. Learn to become sensitive at will and

Psychometry

A step by step guide

This is one of the finest ways to develop psychic ability using concentration and contemplation. Following the principle that we live in a sea of mind energy which is impressed by all matter in creation, the most simple physical object must have thought energy within it. The science of radionics has been developed to study the properties of different minerals and metals to discover which are the most conducive to different types of mind energy. Gold, silver and precious stones are particularly effective in storing psychic energy.

The psychometrist uses this principle by concentrating and contemplating on an object, such as a ring, watch or bracelet which has been worn regularly by one person only. Their thoughts and feelings will be registered firmly within the object and the psychometrist will be able to discern much about them purely by holding it in his hand.

To practise psychometry, take such an object from somebody, preferably someone you do not know at all well, hold it between the index finger and thumb of both hands and start to concentrate upon it briefly. Then swiftly move into a more contemplative state allowing the mind energy contained in the object to come to you. Start to observe the thoughts, feelings, pictures and even sounds which float through your mind. Since you are learning, it is perfectly acceptable to ask questions of the other person to see how accurate you are.

By practising this you will learn the difference between a genuine psychic impression and just your imagination. When you correctly identify an image or thought which you could not have known about consciously, remember the sensation that you experienced so that you can discriminate between this and just a flight of the imagination.

Gradually you will become more and more accurate at this practice, which can be great fun as well as an extremely effective method of psychic development. You may even start to gain impressions not only about the present and past of the owner of the object, but about their future as well, which indicates that you are becoming clairvoyant. You will then be tuning into the sea of energy within which all life exists.

insensitive at will. You will get to the stage where you can feel the true thoughts of your friends, the radiations from your friend's dining room or from the cup that you drink coffee out of which has been used by your dear in-laws an hour before. This faculty must be turned on and off, and you must have strict control of yourself. Self-discipline is essential if you are going to develop psychic abilities. If you have self-discipline, you can safely develop them and they will be of tremendous help to you, and very often to your friends who may need your help. You will get to the stage where you will be able to take hold of a letter, for instance, and not only read what it says, which is one thing, but read what it really says, which is often something else. You can imagine what a tremendous help that could really be to you. Do not make any great decisions in your life based on the use of this faculty until you know that it is really working within you.

You are activating, not so much the tips of your fingers but certain psychic centres within the body, which give you the ability to feel, through the tips of your fingers, subtle emanations. You are making *prana* flow in a certain way, through the subtle nervous centre of the body, and then you are beginning to bring together this pranic flow to put pressure on certain psychic centres. The key is practice, practice and more practice. That is all it takes.

The best items to practise on should have been worn for a long time by someone, because their vibrations will be really impressed in there. I would suggest something with fairly flat surfaces. The stone in a ring can be extremely difficult if it is cut like a diamond, but if it is a big flat stone it is easier. Some plastic is fairly inert to vibrations, whereas other more natural substances, like pearls for instance, would be more open to receive vibrations. Pure metal such as gold or silver is easy to psychometrise since it is very absorbent to vibrations. Glass is very absorbent because it is made of silicon and would be an easy thing to practise on. Wearing apparel can be difficult unless it is something like silk. A gold watch, or one with some gold plating round it, would be easier than a steel watch. Keys are sometimes good, but anything worn near the skin is ideal to practise on.

Pendulum Dowsing

Another excellent way to develop your psychic and intuitive abilities is pendulum dowsing.

The pendulum is a radionic instrument which can be used as a focal point for psychic energies. The general belief in metaphysical circles in England used to be that the dowser is used as a medium and that their guide or some discarnate entity would cause their hand to move. This is incorrect—it is something which you do. It is a way of proving that the subconscious mind will come up with the answer if you let it. It is an interesting psychic experiment. Treat it as such, but do not let the pendulum rule your life. You can make the pendulum say what you want it to say quite easily, but if this is the case, why bother to use a pendulum in the first place?

It is a good idea to obtain a little case in which to keep your pendulum so that you are the only person to handle it. The best kind of pendulum to have is the simplest kind. It may not be the least expensive, but definitely the simplest. The bobbin at the end can be made from carved beechwood or, if you want to be a little more exotic, sandalwood is good. Some people use ebony and I have also heard of jet being used. You do see pendulums that are very expensive with all kinds of little stones and crystals, but I feel that one should keep them as simple as possible. I think the majority of people would do better with beechwood. The best shape to have them carved is semi-conical, coming down to a definite point. Pear-shaped with a definite point will suffice as well. When suspended, the bobbin must be correctly balanced so that it does not flop over to one side. Do not use lead as a metal for your bobbin, and do not use any material known to be radioactive, such as something painted with luminous paint. In order to connect your thread to the bobbin, I suggest some loop or hook made of German silver which is quite cheap. The suspending thread must be made out of the purest silk obtainable. There are other things, like animal hair which is often used, but you cannot beat pure silk thread.

Remember, with a pendulum all you have is a bobbin on the end of a piece of cord, so do not let the pendulum run your life. It is, however, a very good way of tapping the knowledge which is already in your subconscious or intuitive mind.

Learn to Dowse with a Pendulum

and find out how it works for you

I cannot be categorical and say that everyone must hold it in their right hand, but generally it should be. You will have to find out for yourself. You will also have to experiment as to what length of cord you use—some people find it works better with a longer cord than others. It is a good idea to put a small knot in the position on the cord where it is best for you to hold it. When people are really experienced with the pendulum they have several knots at different distances down the cord and then run their finger down the cord, catching each knot with their thumbnail and they get to know what length is best for the pendulum for different uses. What suits one person may not suit another, but instinctively you will discover which length is best for you.

The correct way to hold a pendulum is to have the elbow higher than the wrist. You hold the cord, at your chosen length, between the thumb and index finger, with the other fingers spread out (see illustration). The idea is to have a downward flow of energy right through the elbow, arm, wrist into the fingers and down the pendulum cord. It is general for the pendulum to swing clockwise for "yes", counterclockwise for "no" and neither for "not sure". You can ascertain whether an answer "yes" for you is clockwise or anti-clockwise by asking something you know the answer to.

Take your pendulum and hold it in the right hand; then take your left hand and close it over the bobbin so as to "kill" any vibration which may be on it, and then hold the pendulum over something you already know the answer to. For instance, you could hold it over hot water and ask the pendulum "is the water hot?" After holding your pendulum over an object, put your other hand round it to cut off the vibration before your next question.

If you give healing and are sensitive, you will find that one of the best ways of using a pendulum is to hold it in one hand while you run the tips of the fingers of the other hand over the object you want to examine. I have seen health checks done in this way. You can pick out one nerve or one muscle on a person with one hand and watch the pendulum swing with the other. Even though you may not know what is wrong, you can detect positive and negative reactions providing you are an expert. Some radionic experts will take a blood spot from a person and put the pendulum over the blood spot to determine what health remedies are required.

How to hold it correctly

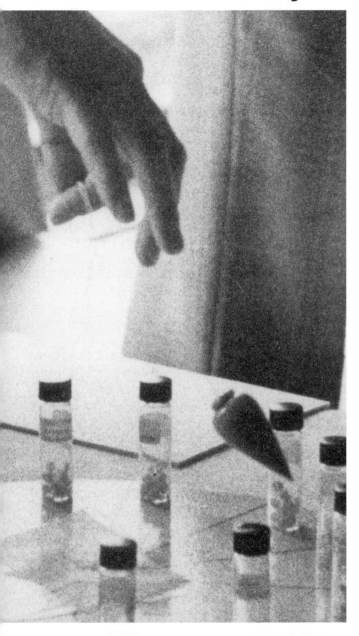

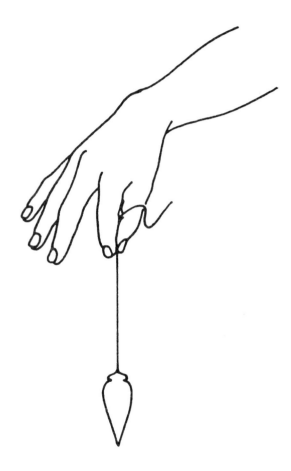

The Aura and Psychic Centres

Whereas emphasis in the west has been on practicality and physical achievement, the eastern tradition has been always associated with inner attainment. The yoga philosophy of India, the Daoist philosophy of China and the oriental martial arts schools, focus on the limitless potential within the individual and tap it through one method or another. As we enter the new millennium, the spiritual nature of man is becoming better understood in the west as well.

We not only inhabit a physical body, but also a psychic body, known as the aura. This is an energy body composed of spiritual or etheric matter. It extends several inches beyond the physical body and contains within it psychic centres, or chakras (see illustration), and an interconnecting network of channels known in Sanskrit as the *nadis*. Indian writings refer to no less than 72,000 of these *nadis*, interconnecting major and minor psychic centres to produce a constant flow of etheric energy within and around the aura.

Our mental, physical and emotional states result from these fluctuating energy patterns

Like water going down a plughole: the psychic centres in the aura are vortices that suck energy in or send it out.

within the aura. As the energies pass through this psychic nervous system, so we experience feelings and thoughts. In due course these energetic manifestations of feeling and thought manifest at a physical level—hence psychosomatic conditions which medical experts are agreed nowadays are the cause of most diseases and ailments. This interconnecting system of psychic centres and nadis is designed to bring a positive, spiritual, transmuting effect within the individual.

The psychic centres are really vortices within the etheric structure. These vortices of power allow energy to flow through the aura and the subtle nervous system. They allow the individual, as a conscious being, to use this power for good or evil.

To give an illustration of what they look like, you will notice that when taking the plug out of the bathtub, the escaping water creates a whirlpool over the plug hole. It goes down and tapers off to a point. A psychic centre is shaped rather like this. It is virtually a whirlpool in which certain energies are drawn in or, in some cases, radiated outward through the aura which is around the body. These centres taper off to very thin channels which are joined onto the spinal column. Every major psychic centre is joined to the spine in this way (see illustrations). The secondary psychic centres are joined to the spine also, but more indirectly through the nervous system. If you imagine these centres like multi-coloured whirlpools, starting at a point on the spinal column and coming right out in the aura, like a flower, through the physical body to the

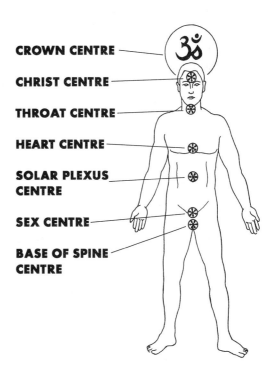

THE MAJOR PSYCHIC CENTRES

CROWN CENTRE

CHRIST CENTRE

THROAT CENTRE

HEART CENTRE

SOLAR PLEXUS CENTRE

SEX CENTRE

BASE OF SPINE CENTRE

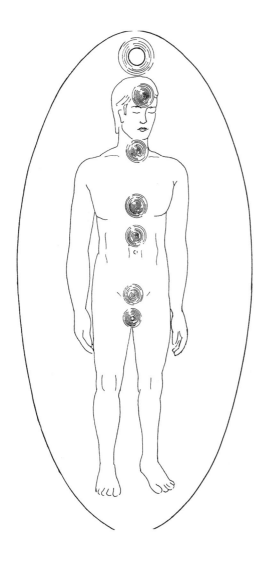

The aura is our subtle body and reflects everything about us –
our health, our mind, our emotions and our spiritual
development. Roughly ovoid in shape, it contains the psychic
centres, through which energy enters and leaves it.

front, you will have some idea of what a
psychic centre looks like.

Without them, we could not possibly live.
We could not think; we would not have any
consciousness at all. None of us could be
here on this Earth, or even in manifestation. The psychic centres are the most
valuable things in all of our existence, with
the exception, naturally, of life itself. They
are not the spirit—the God spark—but
essential tools used by the God spark in
order to bring to us all an opportunity to
gain experience in a material world.

As vortices of energy, or floodgates, they
can be opened or closed. If you look at an
ordinary person psychically, you will see
that his psychic centres are not particularly bright or glowing as they should be.
Whereas, the person who thinks deeply
and works in a metaphysical way, whether
they are aware of it or not, has his or her
psychic centres glowing brightly, just like
orbs of multi-coloured light, or like centres
in which multi-coloured lights move
around at a tremendous speed.

I will give you an idea of the colossal
velocities here. The forces in the christ
centre are known by some adepts to move
round in this great vortex of power at
above four million times the speed of

light. Light itself moves at a velocity on this Earth of 186,000 miles per second (299,274 kilometres per second). Multiply that by four million and a few more and you have some idea of the velocities of the tremendous energies which operate through the christ centre. This should give you all a little idea of these great whirlpools, or flood gates, of energy. They are really a contact with all the forces outside of mankind, as well as being able to give mankind the secrets of that which is within himself.

Starting from the top, the crown chakra is the main psychic centre of the human organism. Then comes the christ centre—some people call it the third eye. When this centre is open you have perfect vision. Your vision is not governed by a time frame. You can see the past, present and future as happening in the now. There are very few people on Earth, despite their claims, who have this centre fully opened. This centre cannot be opened by surgical operations, despite the claim of some so-called lamas. It can only be opened in one way, and that is by strict control of the *kundalini*. When "she" rises from the base centre and lodges in the christ centre and even above, you have control over all the psychic centres. You are on Earth for one

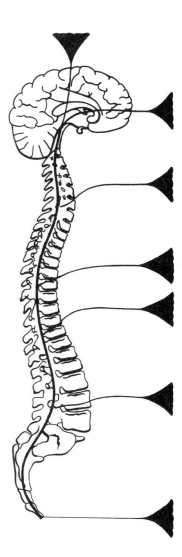

CROWN CHAKRA

CHRIST CENTRE

THROAT CENTRE

HEART CENTRE

SOLAR PLEXUS CENTRE

SEX CENTRE

BASE OF THE SPINE

reason: to control the power of *kundalini*. There is no truth higher than this, nor can there be. Do not take my word for it, read the Akashic Records, where it is written plainly in the universal language to last forever. When *kundalini* is risen to this centre, you are a master.

Then comes the throat centre. When the power of the kundalini is lodged in the throat centre, you are a master of sound. Although you may not be able to speak them, you can understand all the languages on the Earth and you will be initiated into the only real language—of "TUL". This language varies with the time-frame continuum as it moves and evolves, so a phrase in "TUL" at 20 minutes past seven one evening could not possibly be expressed in the same way at 10 minutes past eight the same evening.

The heart centre comes next. When the *kundalini* lodges in the heart centre you are capable of levitation and also, you hear the great sound made by the tremendous in- and outflow of energies through the heart centre. It is rather similar to the sound which comes from the sun every 32 minutes of the day and night. This tremendous gong-like sound comes from the heart centre.

Next comes the solar plexus centre. This is the battery of the human body. Just as there is an electric battery in your car, so we have a solar plexus centre. Lower down is the sex centre, and down at the bottom of the base of the spine is the lowest centre of all. The base centre is joined through the aura, through a subtle nerve system, to the base of the spine.

As well as the psychic centres and nadic channels, there is another great force within our auric body—the greatest of all the forces we can contact within ourselves—the *kundalini*. This was depicted in Sanskrit writings as a three-and-a-half-coiled serpent which can be raised up the nadic channel within the spine known as *susumna* by an advanced yogic practitioner. Even inside susumna there was a channel described as being a fraction of the width of a hair, known as *citrini*, and it is through this that the *kundalini* rises. This "serpent power", as it is known, uncoils itself and gradually enters each psychic centre in turn. As it does so, mind consciousness on all levels is opened up to the yogi, or yogini (female yogi). When Jesus was tempted by the serpent—described in the Bible as being satan—with great powers over the dominions, unlimited wealth and so on, it was not an allegorical tale but an actual fact. Had he

The Seashore Practice

An exercise to bring peace, harmony and clairvoyant visions

Sit on a hard-backed chair with your spine straight and palms facing downwards just above the knees. You may prefer to adopt an *asana* such as *padma* – it doesn't matter how you sit as long as the spine is straight and you feel alert, yet relaxed. Close the eyes.

Take few deep breaths and detach from the hustle and bustle of the outside world.

Imagine that you are standing on a beach, with golden, perfectly smooth sand beneath your feet. You are wearing your favourite clothes. Your hair is being gently rustled by a light, refreshing breeze. Look up at the beautiful blue sky, flecked with the odd tuft of cloud, and feel the warmth of the sun against your cheeks. Now gaze out to sea – a calm, blue sea, which reflects the bright sunlight. Try not to involve any people in the scene.

Now relax your concentration slightly and just let whatever is going to happen, happen. The sea may become a little rougher, the wind a little stronger, the sand a little less smooth, or the whole scene may change completely – just allow this to happen. These changes symbolise your near future. Don't dwell on any one thing for too long, just observe, and don't worry if at first you don't understand what the changes mean.

After having done this for a while, use all the power of your imagination to turn the scene back to exactly how it was with the perfect sand, the bright sun, the calm sea etc., then gently bring yourself back to the physical world around you.

This practice is deceptively simple—it has a deep mystical significance and, if done correctly, will bring a sense of calm and balance, and even enhance your intuitive awareness, enabling you to see the future and change your karmic pattern.

raised this serpent power up the front of the body instead of the spine, thereby activating the psychic centres (or at least some of them) in an unnatural way, he could have gained great powers that could manifest through magical practice and give him political and financial success. Hence his admonishment, "Get thee behind me, satan!", or in other words, let the serpent power travel up the back of the spine through citrini in a natural way, and open up the psychic centres in accordance with metaphysical law. This would bring spiritual power and influence to be used only for the benefit of others—such as tremendous healing abilities and wisdom.

When we breathe, we take in two sorts of energy. We must remember that everything in nature has an opposite pole—that unless it had an opposite pole, it could not exist. In this context I mean the term negative as an opposite pole to positive, not anything bad. We draw in energy through the left nostril which is of a negative nature; we draw in energy through the right nostril which is of a positive nature. These two streams of energy come up and over, down each side of the spine, cross over at the base of the spine, change polarity and come back up again, being dispensed throughout the whole of the subtle nervous system, of which there are reputedly 72,000 main arteries. If we impose a control over these two streams of energy and do not allow them to come up each side of the spine, but instead try to bring them up through the centre of the spinal column, then they directly activate all psychic centres.

In the spine we have what is tantamount to a cyclotron. Outside in the atmosphere there is an inexhaustible supply of energy. At the base of the spine, in the bottom psychic centre, we have an energy referred to in the ancient books as the fire of *kundalini*. It is called the Goddess and is like a three-and-a-half-coiled serpent which lies sleeping in *Muladhara*, or the base of the spine psychic centre. Now if we bring these two great forces together with sufficient intensity—the energy outside of our bodies, the universal life force, and the energy latent at the bottom of the spine—we have something tantamount to a minor atomic explosion. This explosion releases the fire of *kundalini*, or primordial force, upwards—not each side of the spine, through the left hand channel (*ida*) or the right hand channel (*pingala*), and certainly not through the front of the psychic centres, but up through the tiny channel in the centre of the spinal column (*susumna*). **The channel within *susumna* is called *citrini*, and is about one hundredth part of a human hair in breadth. It is extremely subtle.**

There is one major difference of emphasis between the eastern approach to personal development and the western approach. Sri Patanjali, who is regarded as the father of Raja Yoga, the yoga of mind control, quite openly advocated suppression of mental impulses so that a vacuum would be created. Into this would then come great wisdom and knowledge through the raising of the *kundalini* and the activation of the higher psychic centres. In the west, on the other hand, there has been a tendency to frown upon all forms of suppression on the basis that they cause unnatural subconscious blockages and it is far better to get emotional and mental impulses "out of your system". In fact, both these approaches are valid in different ways at different times. All great truth contains paradox. Dr. King once made the following statement:

Truth has two poles. It must have in order to balance. At the exact intersecting point of positive and negative lines of mental force, consciousness is produced. Consciousness is capable of that faculty of discrimination which eventually produces truth.

This statement, I believe, is worthy of your meditation. I have certainly learned much from these words over the years. It applies to all areas of great teaching and indicates a fundamental balance which runs through life: the *yin* and the *yang* of thought.

While it is certainly true that suppression can cause blockages, at the same time, the getting-things-out-of-your-system approach can only empower the very thoughts and emotions you are trying to eliminate. In essence, the individual journey of the spiritual nature of every man and woman on Earth is a journey of transmutation of all thought, all emotion and all energy up to its highest level

Prana is the life of the atom and the vitality of the most elevated inspiration of the enlightened saint.

Dr. George King

The Fourth Initiation
Harnessing the One Energy

Science and Energy

Everything and everyone is composed of energy. All life is an expression of energy in different forms. This not only applies to the physical level, it also applies to the mental and spiritual levels. Chaos theory says that the breath of wind caused by a butterfly's wings in Sumatra can cause a series of consequences which finally result in a hurricane devastating islands in the Caribbean. It is true that all events are interconnected, but at a much deeper level than chaos theory suggests, for that only deals with the physical effects of this interconnection. Mystics believe that there is a universal supply of energy directed by a supreme, creative force. Such a belief implies a complete oneness through all creation and modern scientists are increasingly embracing this as a

fundamental concept. Science is, after all, the study of relationships.

Chaos theory says that the flapping of a butterfly's wings on one side of the world can cause a hurricane on the other.

In ancient Greece, the legendary story of Archimedes, a genius in both mathematics and physics, provides a good example of this. He was asked by King Hieron II of Syracuse to find out whether a goldsmith had substituted silver for gold in making his new crown. Thinking about this problem while getting into a bathtub, he realised that anything put into the tub of water would displace its own volume. This, of course, was a far more important discovery than the value of the king's crown. Then followed the famous incident when he leapt out of his bath and ran naked through the streets of Syracuse to the king's palace shouting: "Eureka!" which means "I have found", or "I have discovered". In this case it was the relationship between mass and volume which enabled a measurement to take place.

Centuries later, in 1665, the 23-year-old Isaac Newton, while lying in the orchard of Woolsthorpe in Lincolnshire, saw an apple fall to the ground. Rather like Archimedes, he had an instant realisation about the laws of science. Incidentally, when asked later how he had discovered the laws of gravity, Newton replied that he had been thinking about them continually. It is necessary to work very hard to think, to deduce, and use the powers of the mind, but great realisations often come in a flash of inspiration. By seeing this apple fall to the earth, he suddenly understood the gravitational force which attracts planetary bodies to each other and keeps the cosmos as we know it in balance. He found that bodies attract each other with a force inversely proportional to the square of the distance between them, and so linked together a relationship between the quantities of mass, force and distance which was to be one of the foundations of physics from that day forth.

At the beginning of the 20th century the Newtonian view of an ordered cosmos of fixed relationships started to be, if not overturned, at least questioned, and found to be incomplete. Max Planck, the father of quantum mechanics, discovered in 1900 that subatomic particles do not operate in the ordered wave motion that all scientists had assumed they would—as light, sound and radio waves do, for example. Instead they appear to operate haphazardly in groups of energy, or quanta as they became known. Einstein, regarded by most as the greatest scientific genius of the period, worked long and hard on this problem and, rather like Archimedes and Newton, came up with his theory of relativity in a flash of inspiration while daydreaming about the crescent moon. This concerned relationships again—in this case between light and mass. The very idea of relativity suggests interconnection.

Now Einstein's theories are being shown to be incomplete as new things are being discovered and realised about the universe. It is no longer universally accepted that the speed of light is the ultimate velocity. The remarkable thing though, is that despite all these revisions of science, which is constantly being updated, an interconnecting oneness is ever present. If it were not, the universe could not exist in its current form. Take, for example, the discovery by astronomers using powerful radio telescopes, that there is far more mass in the universe than had been assumed. Analysing the perturbations in the orbits of planets and the behaviour of planetary bodies beyond this solar system, and building up a model of the universe, they realised that for the laws of gravity as we know them to operate, there must be far more mass in the universe than we have detected. This has led to the current belief in "dark matter", or undetectable mass. Some theorise about the possible existence of negative mass. It is believed by scientists that every subatomic particle in nature has an associated anti-particle which has the exact opposite properties. Incidentally, this is not too far from

The 23-year-old Isaac Newton, while lying in the orchard of Woolsthorpe in Lincolnshire, saw an apple fall to the ground. Rather like Archimedes, he had an instant realisation about the laws of science.

Einstein came up with his theory of relativity while daydreaming about the crescent moon.

Great realisations often come in a flash of inspiration.

A spiral galaxy similar to our own

The "big bang" theory of how the universe started parallels the ancient Hindu philosophy, which spoke about the "out-breathing" of matter and the "in-breathing" when it returns to its Source again.

the ancient Chinese mystic teaching that the universe is composed of the two balancing forces of *yin* and *yang*.

These antiparticles combine to form so-called antimatter, with the theoretical possibility of antiplanets, antistars and even antigalaxies. Samuel Ting of the European particle physics laboratory was quoted in the British publication, *The New Scientist*, on August 3rd, 1996, as saying, "There is no compelling reason why the universe should be made of matter rather than an equal mix of matter and antimatter." When matter and antimatter meet, according to modern physicists, they annihilate each other. Some speculate that antimatter would also have the effect of causing an object to exceed the speed of light and even arrive at a new destination before it had left the original one. Such concepts take Star Trek technology out of the realms of science fiction and make it a real possibility for the future.

Theories about the nature and behaviour of the universe are ever changing, but it is generally believed that the so-called "big bang" theory is an accurate description of how the universe started. This states that there was a still void out of which emerged massive forces of mass, heat and light expanding outward at the speed of light. This big bang created the planetary bodies and the universe as we know it. This theory postulates that the universe is ever expanding until the force of gravity from its collective mass overcomes the kinetic energy of the initial "bang" and will grow and grow until something causes either overheating or the contraction of mass created by the explosion of stars and planets. This would bring about a contraction of the universe, until it possibly caused another big bang event or until it completely disappeared. This overall description parallels exactly the ancient Hindu philosophy which spoke about the "out-breathing" of matter and the "in-breathing" when it returns to its Source again.

With the discovery of dark matter, or invisible matter, has come the concept of white dwarfs, black holes, and more recently, cosmic wormholes. These concepts, which preoccupy the minds of many modern theoretical physicists, concern small areas in space in which an extraordinary density of mass exists. These extraordinary densities can be caused by massive stars, much larger than our sun, collapsing upon themselves through their own gravity, the dissolution of planetary bodies and even stars. Aided and abetted by the commercial imaginations of Hollywood producers, gruesome concepts of black holes emerged as some kind of evil force absorbing all life which came anywhere near their gravitational pull into a deathly void. Cosmic wormholes are looked upon more favourably. It is believed that in these extraordinary concentrations of dense mass, or so-called negative mass, since gravity exists proportionally to mass, the forces of gravity are immense. Since motion also exists relative to gravity, and time itself exists relative to velocity, it is theorised that in a cosmic wormhole it is possible to traverse immense distances of time and space almost instantaneously. A spacecraft could enter a cosmic wormhole, which would have the property of a tunnel, taking the spacecraft to the other end of the universe in a very short space of time. It would even be possible to travel through time into the future or the past.

Such concepts are no longer the prerogative of science fiction but are being seriously worked on in university departments around the world. All of them depend on relationships between mass, gravity, time and velocity. The further they are taken, so increasingly a oneness throughout creation becomes apparent. There is a relationship between all things: space, time, consciousness and even moral issues. Science, philosophy and religion start to merge into an interconnected oneness. Everything is an expression of energy. Even mass, as Einstein said, is only energy manifesting in a certain way. Space and time only exist relative to energy.

We are living in an energy zone. That zone is determined by the frequency of vibration upon which we operate, mentally, physically and in every other way. This explains all psychic phenomena and may ultimately explain much about so-called invisible matter. Understanding energy provides the key to understanding life, because all things can be seen as forms of energy, even mind. Thoughts are as much energy as physical actions, the only difference being that they are operating on different frequency levels. The 1933 Nobel Laureate Paul Dirac hit upon something which shared common ground with the great mystical philosophies of the Chinese *Dao De Jing* and the Hindu Upanishads. A paper published by Richard F. Plzak, Jr. in 1973 summarised Dirac's finding, when he said this: "All matter is created out of some imperceptible substratum and the creation of matter leaves behind it a 'hole' in this substratum which appears as antimatter. Now, this substratum itself is not accurately described as material, since it uniformly fills all space and is undetectable by any observation. In a sense, it

appears as NOTHINGNESS—immaterial, undetectable, and omnipresent. But it is a peculiarly material form of nothingness, out of which all matter is created." How close this is to the philosophy of Lao Zi, who said in the *Dao De Jing*: "There is a thing inherent and natural which existed before heaven and earth. Motionless and fathomless, it stands alone and never changes; it pervades everywhere and never becomes exhausted." Both these statements, though separated by two and a half millennia, indicate in different terminology the existence of a universal supply of invisible energy out of which matter is created. Something which pre-dates manifestation as we know it and yet is ever present. This is the universal supply of natural energy which flows through every level and frequency of existence in the cosmos.

The Sanskrit word *prana* is the term used in the Vedas to describe this natural universal supply of energy from which manifestation is brought into being. *Prana* was said to exist in *akasha*, the Sanskrit word which means ether. The ethers of space include but go beyond the purely physical level. They contain every aspect of life, including mind, which is only a specific pattern placed upon the energy. Life is really, then, an energy zone which is itself broken down into many other zones, all depending which frequency the natural energies are vibrating at. All this suggests a force greater than we can understand at this stage of our evolution: a life force. Every object, animate or inanimate, has a mind which causes the constituents of its energy patterns to vibrate in a certain way, thereby making them the objects they are.

According to the Hindu *Bhagavata Purana*, all gross matter is generated by transformations of ether. We can see modern scientists starting to glimpse this type of metaphysical concept, such as a current theory of geometrodynamics, which holds that all material particles are simply twists or deformations of space-time. Both the Bhagavata Purana and some modern scientific theories imply that matter is directly connected to ether. If you can manipulate the ethers of space, you can manipulate gross matter. This is the key to understanding the age-old quest for mind over matter.

Much as the scientific community might frown at the very idea, it has much in common with the mystical quest for truth. For one thing, it is constantly up-dating and reviewing its findings, much as the mystic moves from stage to stage, initiation to initiation, in his unfolding realisation of higher knowledge. It is an evolutionary process during which each facet of truth takes on new and deeper meanings as the mystic progresses. Scientists are often less honest though. There is a kind of optimistic amnesia when people study the most up-to-date scientific findings. They conveniently forget that throughout all history science has been revised. What is considered the orthodox view of life on this Earth and beyond in one era, may be regarded in a few hundred years as an absurd mistake, an almost laughable primitivism.

The whole concept of higher vibratory life is absolutely crucial to the study of cosmology. Scientists studying the possibility of life on other planets have often tended to assume that it would function like life on Earth, thereby virtually ruling out life of a different or higher kind. If you or I could not live on Mars, Venus, Jupiter or any other planet, according to this doctrine, then neither could anybody else. It is only recently that certain scientists, such as the Astronomer Royal Sir Martin Rees have started to speculate that there could be life "not as we know it".

To the metaphysician, of course, if it is possible for higher life forms to exist on this world—people who have died and inhabit soul or astral bodies—then it is just as logical to suggest that people can live on other planets in higher bodies.

It is also worth remembering that in ancient Greece, from which much of our science and philosophy derives, the differentiation between mind and matter or spirit and matter, came as late as the 5th century BC when Democritus said: "Nothing exists except atoms and space; everything else is opinion." Before that, in the 6th century BC, there was a school of philosophy in ancient Greece known as the Milesian school. They were called Hylozoists, which literally means, "those who think matter is alive". They saw no distinction between animate and inanimate, spirit and matter. One of their most brilliant thinkers, Anaximander, saw the universe as a single organism which was supported by *pneuma*, literally, the cosmic breath, in the same way as the human body is supported by air. This *pneuma* has much in common with the concept of universal life forces which has dominated mysticism in the east and the west under different names for centuries.

Universal Life Forces

Just as the physical body has an aura, so do all parts of creation. We live in a sea of energy, or *prana*.

Every breath we take, every mouthful of liquid or solid we consume, is charged with that vital force known in the east as *prana*. In fact, *prana* is the sum total of all cosmic energy. It is the energy which enables you to bend your little finger; it is the energy which, manifesting as gravitation, causes a passing meteor to be drawn into the orbit of a planetary body. Without *prana*, there could be no motion of any kind and all cosmic manifestation would fade into its original state of dark, motionless potential; for *prana* is the energy which brings forth the realisation of the original possibilities into the numerous phases of activated manifestation which constitute the whole of cosmic creation.

***Prana* is the life of the atom and the vitality of the most elevated inspiration of the enlightened saint. All creation revolves upon an energy axis—*prana*. Ten thousand words could be written about *prana* without describing it in its entirety, yet one word is sufficient for the thinking man. *Prana* is Life.**

Although everything contains *prana*, it is in its most accessible form in the air we breathe. Even though it is neither the oxygen nor the nitrogen, it is the energy which vitalises these, for without *prana*, neither the oxygen nor the nitrogen atoms could exist but would still be an inert possibility in the mind of the Creator.

If no mental or material thing can exist without the vitalising factor of pranic vibration and this vibration charges every molecule of air we breathe, it can easily be seen how important are correct breathing methods.

In the west, doctors regard the oxygen and nitrogen and their absorption into the blood circulatory system, as the primary function of breathing; but for centuries the occultist has known otherwise. He has admitted that deep breathing of fresh, clean air fills the bloodstream with oxygenated particles which are pumped by the heart to every extremity of the human body, thereby feeding every cell and causing much waste toxic matter to be consumed.

But this is only one aspect of the all-important action of breathing. The yogi calls this the negative aspect. The positive aspect—and the most important one—is the direct absorption of vital pranic energy by the nervous and brain systems, without which they could not exist, never mind function properly.

In case some readers should confuse *prana* with spirit, a few words about the essential relationship will not be amiss. Imagine a radiant, angelic being, clothed in the dazzling white robes of purity, riding in a chariot pulled by two strong, fleet horses through the golden gates of a magnificent temple. This angelic being, beautiful beyond all description, is symbolic of the Spark of Divinity within you—the spirit. The will he exerts through his hands over his horses represents the part played by your soul; his guiding hands, your mind, and the powerful horses, *prana*; while the chariot symbolises your physical body and the temple, his destination, represents God, which is the eventual destination of every soul. This is a poor illustration but it is hoped that it may at least serve to explain the part played by the spirit and by *prana*, which is the vital energy that is used by the Divine Spirit through the will in the journey through evolution.

Even the most conservative thinkers will admit they believe that all creation is passing through a slow, steady stage of evolution. If we believe in the evolution of man, we must go one stage further and admit that, before evolution is possible, involution must have taken place. How can absolute perfection evolve any higher than absolute perfection? God is Absolute Perfection and therefore above any evolutionary necessity or possibility.

The spirit, as an individualised particle of God, must be completely perfect, and therefore beyond the possibility of evolution, unless the Creator had seen fit in the beginning to involve each individualised Divine Spark of Himself. This, then, is what happened. In the beginning, there was silent, motionless perfection, which was God. Then God, as the Creator, saw fit to involve, or wrap up, each specific part of Himself in matter; so we had the great out-breathing, the result of which was all manifestation on every plane of existence—the whole unit of cosmic manifestation.

Next we have the great control (the yogis call it *pranayama*) of the breath of God, during which time the spirit passed further and further into matter according to the plan of the Divine Architect. Then we have the great in-breathing, during which time the spirit throws off the binding shackles of mind and matter and evolves until it is God again.

This is the logical explanation of how creation was made. No man knows why. For some reason, beyond even the capacity of our deepest meditations, God saw fit to involve Himself and thereby necessitate the system of evolution.

These simple words provide some reasons for the past, present and future existence of everything. There is not a religion on Earth which does not say the same thing in different ways. Christianity speaks of satan and the falling away through temptation. Call it what you like, the truth remains that this wrapping up of the perfect Flame of Divinity did take place and self-conscious man realises, most times dimly, that he has to make the long, tedious journey through countless lives and dimensions back to the Source of all things, which is union, or yoga. *Prana* is the energy which enables this journey to be made.

The Chinese called it *qi (ch'i)*. The Polynesians believed it had been harnessed to erect the Easter Island statues and called it *mana*. Esoteric Orders in the Middle Ages connected with the Knights Templar and the Teutonic Knights knew about it under different names. Alchemists like Paracelsus and Van Helmont revealed it publicly in the same period, referring to it as *munis* and *magnale magnum* respectively. Von Reichenbach referred to "odic" or "odylic" force. Radiesthesia exponents talk about an "etheric force" and theosophists an "astral light". In the 20th century, L.E. Eeman referred to an "X-Force" and William Reich to "orgone energy". Soviet parapsychologists talked about "bioplasmic energy" and "psychotronic energy". Of course, not all their definitions are the same, but the central concept of an all-pervasive energy throughout the cosmos runs through many cultures.

The ancient Egyptians used to harness this natural energy through the shape power of the pyramids, as did the early inhabitants of South America where pyramids have also been discovered. Incidentally, some of the parallels between structures found in South America and Egypt are uncanny. The widely held view that the Great Pyramid of Giza was really a place of initiation is taken one step further by those who believe that it was also a radionic instrument. The shape power of its structure created energy fields which brought about an elevated state of consciousness in the initiate under certain conditions. Numerous experiments have shown that the pyramid does have powers, which can only be caused by its ability to harness the universal life forces in a potent, natural state and bring about a change not only to the subtle aspects of matter, but also to their material counterpart. Some of the claims made about the effect of putting physical articles inside even a small four-sided pyramid are the following: tarnished jewellery and coins have been polished; polluted water has been purified; milk has remained fresh for several days and eventually turned straight into yogurt instead of becoming sour; meat and eggs have been dehydrated; flowers have dehydrated but retained their form and colour; cuts, bruises and burns have healed faster; plants have grown more quickly; the taste of wine, coffee and fruit juice has improved; and people have had mystical experiences of one kind or another. The Egyptians were very aware of the importance of the alignment of cosmic forces and, above all, the profound influence on all life of the sun.

All the energy in this solar system comes from and through the sun. This is one of the reasons why many ancient civilisations worshipped it as the one source of all energy. As far as we are concerned it could virtually be regarded as God, because it provides all that

All the energy in this solar system comes from and through the sun.

This is one of the reasons why many ancient civilisations worshipped it as the one source of all energy.

we are, including the molecules and atoms of our own physical bodies. From Zoroastrianism to tribal groups in deepest Africa and South America, reverence for the celestial orb has been common. Worship of the sun is no primitive belief—it is a logical recognition of the greatest and most divine object with which we have any kind of contact. So if you wish to identify one aspect of creation as the life force above all others, it would be the sun. But in the totality of the universe, this force goes even beyond one solar system or even one galaxy. The universal life forces are the energies of the Creator Itself and, according to mystical and occult writings, they pervade the entire ethers of space.

As long ago as the 1920s, the great scientist Sir Oliver Lodge rocked the world's scientific community by proposing that matter is only a manifestation of ether. In a lecture entitled Energy, delivered in Leeds, England on September 6th, 1927, which was internationally reported in such newspapers as *The New York Times* and *The Chicago Tribune*, he said: "It seems to me that there is a guiding and directing principle *ad extrema*, which interacts with the material of the physical universe but is not of it." He went on to say that electrical charges are really in the ether. Only when electrons cease to move do they revolve around one another and form the atoms of matter, which then constitute oceans, rocks, planets and human beings. In other words, he saw a transition between the etheric world and the physical world—though he expressed it in the scientific terminology of his day. Ether is an absolutely vital concept. It is regarded by mystics as the fifth element because it is the one that materialists ignore. They are only familiar with the other four: earth, water, fire and air. But really, ether is the most important element, since it is the one in which all others exist. Just as there are five elements throughout all creation, there are also five major *pranas* and five minor *pranas*. In some of the Upanishads (Hindu scripts), reference is made to the *tattvas*, which are the qualities of all things, and again there are five of these. From a mystical point of view it is believed that the Creator blended all life into five perfectly balanced forces producing all aspects of manifestation, not only on this physical frequency, but on all levels of frequency throughout creation. The different etheric levels, determined by the frequency at which they vibrate, are composed of the universal life forces. From these, the Creator brought all manifestation into being.

Energy and Consciousness

Thomas Edison, the great American inventor, was reported in *Harper's Magazine* in February 1890 as saying: "I do not believe that matter is inert, acted upon by an outside force. To me it seems that every atom is possessed by a certain amount of primitive intelligence. Look at the thousands of ways in which atoms of hydrogen combine with those of other elements, forming the most diverse of substances. Do you mean to say that they do this without intelligence?" The renowned occultist Alice Bailey went even further than this. In her classic mystical work, *The Consciousness of the Atom*, written in 1922, she spoke about the "psyche of the atom", which was an intelligence behind the atom, man, a planet and even a sun. In this she was, as metaphysicians usually are, ahead of the scientific opinion of the day. Later, physicists generally started to accept, from their studies of relativity and quantum physics, that even particles of matter must have some kind of intelligence or direction in order to cooperate with known laws. They are governed by some form of consciousness.

Some modern practitioners of medicine talk about a quantum effect in the healing process. They say that there have been enough cases, rare though they are, of cancer sufferers who, through an attitude of mind, have completely cured themselves, to make a quantum leap in their healing. Illnesses that would normally take a long time to be cured, or be considered incurable, have disappeared almost instantaneously under the direction of mind. This suggests that consciousness is governing and controlling the cells in the body to speed up the healing process under certain conditions. Consciousness pervades the whole of space, controlling the natural energies of creation and bringing perfection and harmony to the universe.

You could describe the journey from one realm to another as a quantum leap, because virtually a leap of consciousness takes place when you move from one level to another. Indeed, the realms of space reflect more than anything else your level of consciousness. On another realm of existence life is entirely physical to the inhabitants of that realm. When you die you pass onto the realm which vibrates at the same level as yourself. This vibratory rate is a reflection of the life force energies associated with your level of consciousness. The possibility exists, not just at the time of death but at any time, to travel through these vibratory rates. I do not just mean through astral projection or "out of body experiences", but by raising your level of consciousness on the realm which you inhabit. This really is the purpose of all life: to use the natural life forces of the universe to raise your own consciousness and ultimately that of creation itself. You could call it the spiritualisation of matter.

The purpose of all life: to use the natural life forces of the universe to raise your consciousness and ultimately that of creation itself. You could call it the spiritualisation of matter.

The Practices of Aetherius

On the following pages we introduce you to the first of several practices delivered through Dr. King by an advanced Cosmic Master known as Aetherius. These are followed by Dr. George King's commentaries.

Dr. King entered a deep, meditative trance condition so that he could be used as a medium to channel them to the world.

Since then, many thousands of people have used these exercises to great effect.

By practising these exercises you will become attuned to the mystical knowledge which lies beneath the surface of material existence and gives it real meaning and purpose.

The Breathing and Recharging Exercise

The Master Aetherius

The primary mento-physical action of terrestrial man is that of breathing. By correct breathing the positive and negative magnetic forces can be equalised within your minds and bodies, thus promoting a mental balance and physical well-being not enjoyed by those who neglect this all-important action.

There are four important times of the day. These times were known to your ancient adepts of Atlantis, and even prior to that, as the times of the holy flow. The great universal energy, manipulated by the sacred Masters on the sun, can be tuned into and absorbed with much benefit during these holy times. The times are: sunrise, midday, sunset and midnight. This knowledge has been closely guarded as a secret for thousands of years, until just recently when, I understand, your most evolved masters of the east were inspired to release the information to the western world. Now I will tell you a secret which only a few belonging to the most advanced schools of occultism know. We are releasing this to the right-thinking man, the open-minded man who has the interests of Terra (Earth) at heart.

At dawn make sure that the breath is flowing up and down the left nostril.

At midday make sure that the breath is flowing up and down the left nostril.

At sunset make sure that the breath is flowing up and down the right nostril.

At midnight make sure that the breath is flowing up and down the right nostril.

This can be done by simply stopping up the opposite nostril with the finger.

This is one part of the cosmic breathing practice—the other part is as follows:

At a time which is convenient to you, lay on a level plane. Be naked if you can—if not, choose light clothing which is not worn as part of your everyday apparel. Obtain some thin, bare copper wire and fashion it in an oval shape around yourself so that the direct contact is made with the nerve centres in the soles of the feet and at the top of the head. Now join another length of wire so that it passes around the chest and back. Make sure that it crosses the chest at the spot just below the chest bone and a corresponding place in the spinal column just between the shoulder blades and about one-and-a-half inches higher up the back, so that it is slightly tilted forward as it were. You lie on this second piece of wire. Now take a few really deep but very slow rhythmic breaths and think into yourself the mighty power of the cosmic system. Try to visualise this vibrant energy sweeping right through your mind and body. If this practice is performed between the times that I have previously stated, then let the breath flow up and down both nostrils together.

A short regular performance of this exercise will not only feed your nervous system but will greatly enhance the activities of your subtler bodies, so that you will gradually become aware of the higher aspects of mind.

My dear friends, if you are going to do these things then please do them properly. If you practise for half an hour today and ten minutes tomorrow, then leave them alone for a month, they will be useless. A few minutes per day, done with interest, good cheer and regularity, will yield great results. You will become aware of the benefits and will be able to protect yourself against the dark forces which are roaming your world at the present time.

The Breathing and Recharging Exercise

Commentary by Dr. George King

It is known to the adepts that *prana* (universal life force) is in its most easily accessible state in the air we breathe. This *prana* enters the left nostril in its negative, feminine, cool state. This is the energy of preservation.

The *prana* which enters the right nostril is in its positive, masculine, warm state. This is the energy of creation.

If these positive and negative energies are correctly balanced within the mental and physical bodies, then the result is as near perfection as mortal man can become upon our Earth. If we breathed correctly all the time, then perfect harmonious balance would be the result. There would be no such thing as insanity or mental deficiency. In all these cases the patient does not breathe an equal number of pranic-charged breaths through each nostril.

The morbid, pessimistic, easily led individuals are those who breathe too frequently through their left nostrils. A cure can be brought about by careful, regular practice of this recharging exercise. Particular attention should be paid to breathing through the right nostril with a view to bringing about a natural balance of forces which enter with the air through the nostrils.

The over-optimistic, highly strung individuals who always perspire easily are breathing too much through their right nostril. This type jumps from subject to subject with great energy, without gaining mastery over anything.

A cure can be brought about by sustained application of the recharging practice. Particular attention should be paid to breathing through the left nostril, with a view to bringing about a natural balance of forces which enter with the air through both nostrils.

Regular practice of this hitherto secret exercise will enhance the results of every other practice contained herein.

The Auric Energy Harmoniser™

A powerful tool to bring about complete auric balance

Dr. King developed the ideas behind the Breathing and Recharging exercise and invented a device known as the Auric Energy Harmoniser (available from The Aetherius Society).

This simple apparatus tends to iron out and cause a more even flow of the energies in the aura, and thereby harmonise your aura. There are many, many forms of frustration, the worst form of which is psychic frustration, from which many people suffer. Whether they have heard of psychic things or not, they suffer from it. The aura is affected by multitudinous things; noise and pollution, for example, affect the aura.

The aura is all-important and you are all-important within this aura. When man is perfect, from an auric point of view, you have a beautiful thing indeed. This struck me more forcibly than anything else when I did meet a really evolved master—the absolutely symmetrical perfection of this being. It is something that an ignoramus like me cannot even begin to describe.

The Auric Energy Harmoniser tends to smooth out the flow of energies in the aura. It is made of very ordinary materials: copper, because it is a positive metal and a good conductor, not only of electricity but also the subtle energies; 24-carat gold, because it is a positive metal and an excellent conductor of subtle energies. If you put a gold bracelet on, it is difficult to get the healing power to travel through your hands. That is why, when we give healing, we take off gold watches or bracelets, because they will stop the power. The gold in the auric energy harmoniser is polished to a very high standard. The apparatus is fairly easy to get in and out of and is completely adjustable, so that if anyone grows another inch in height it can be adjusted. It can last throughout your life.

The copper causes the energy to flow around in a certain direction, creating movement in the aura. The more movement you have in the aura the more you dissipate these "pools" of energy. It works very effectively because it dissipates the pools which manifest as stress points and would otherwise later become psychosomatic conditions. The greatest things in life are the simplest.

Is consciousness the governing force of the universe?

Science deals with the outer limits of the physical world. Already many scientists accept the idea of speeds faster than the speed of light, and increasingly the concept of time travel. They are now knocking at the door of discovering the other dimensions, which metaphysicians know as the other "realms". Scientists have long been searching for a Unified Theory that could embrace Einstein's Theory of Relativity, which has been shown to work in the macrocosmic universe, with quantum theory, which has been shown to predict the microcosmic universe. The current theory which is gaining ever increasing acceptance with modern physicists and has been able to combine the two theories is known as string theory. This theory is new and very complex; however, briefly it postulates that all particles, including electrons, protons and even quarks and gravitons, are actually composed of only one class of object, called a string. As it vibrates in different ways and rates, it forms all the known particles. One interesting mathematical consequence of string theory is that in order to explain all of the known laws, these strings have to exist in at least 10 dimensions—the three spatial dimensions and time, leaving at least six unknown dimensions. Could they be on the verge of discovering the other realms, or planes, at long last?

Many scientists believe in an overriding force or mind governing matter in order to keep it in existence. If there were an extension of the light spectrum, not only beyond that which is visible, but even beyond the so-called invisible light spectrum, it could only move into another frequency of existence. Is there an overlap between sounds which are emitted on the physical plane and sounds which are beyond the limits of physical detection? Do they exist on another realm in space? Can radio waves go beyond the known frequency bands into other levels or spheres of existence? If so, the only governing force behind all these things is consciousness.

The Travelling Practice

The Master Aetherius:

Whenever you travel in a vehicle, try to face the direction of travel. If you cannot do this, then sit so that your right side is facing in the direction you are going. Never ride with your 'back to the engine', as it were, or with your left side facing the direction of travel.

Despite its apparent simplicity, this practice has deep metaphysical implications. The right side of an individual is his sun or positive side. Consequently, when you proceed in this direction, you are travelling into your sun. Likewise, when you face the direction of travel, you automatically signify that you know where you are going and why. Ten minutes' contemplation of the above statements will bring to light some interesting and valuable information.

Despite the surface simplicity of this exercise, it is a vitally important one, as you will soon discover for yourselves. Some students who have practised this with regularity have noted such pronounced success upon their journeys which have an honourable motive, that they would stand rather than face in the wrong direction. This outlook is not born of the wish to become the slaves of ritual but rather their desire to cooperate with a specific, spiritual law, the adherence to which predetermines the result. Neither this, nor any other of these exercises, will work if motivated by purely selfish materialistic gain on the part of those who practise. But knowing the spiritual source from which this practice came, I can state that it will help those whose foremost ambition is to be of service to others. If the flame of this unselfish ambition burns within the sacred chakra of your heart, this and the rest of these sacred practices will provide the essential power to feed this wondrous flame.

What is the relationship between consciousness and matter?

The next step is to understand the relationship between consciousness and matter. They know from quantum physics that there is a force directing the behaviour of particles of matter in order for it to cooperate with the natural laws of the universe. They also know that the mind of an experimenter can actually affect the results of experiments performed on subatomic particles. It is also possible to communicate at a consciousness level with other realms of space. I believe that just as this is the secret to communication with the afterlife, the healing process and other things, it is in fact the key to the whole of science. It is this leap of consciousness which explains the big mysteries of the future. Take, for example, time. We know that time is relative to the mind. We say things like "time passes slowly", or "it seems like only yesterday when I last saw you", when we have not seen someone for years. This is because time is relative to experience, and experience is governed by consciousness. So the key to understanding time, which is the fourth dimension, lies in its relationship to consciousness.

Where does one realm end and another one begin? The same area of space could be occupied with a mountain on one realm of vibrational frequency and a river on another. These are only manifestations which exist around the consciousness of the planet. Ecologists are now postulating that the Earth is indeed a living organism, and in doing so they are hundreds of years behind some so-called primitive tribes who have known this for centuries. The Mother Earth is a living intelligence whose consciousness can control the forces of matter around her on different realms of space.

Basic man regards the energy which he takes into his body as essential only for keeping the body alive, to allow him to go through basic life doing the basic things in his basic environment. But if we begin to look further than basic life, we find that there exists an interrelationship, not only between one life-form and another, but between the worlds, the galaxies and all things which exist—upon all vibrations which can possibly be conceived by The Absolute. Not only do these interrelationships exist, but we are also interrelated with, and directly connected to, that Source from whence we came.

We are a channel through which flows a certain energy. It is up to us how this energy is modified, interfered with or involved, and how this energy is used to help the Whole to evolve. Picture yourself as a collection of highly sensitive, attuned atoms, forming highly sensitive, attuned molecules which form cells. This strange apparatus in which you live has antennae, through which you receive all forms of energy, from the basic form to the highest form. Not only do you receive all forms of energy, but also you transmit all forms of energy.

You might play a beautiful recording through a faulty amplifier, which totally distorts it. When it comes out of the speakers you cannot hear the beautiful recording, you can only hear the distortion caused by the amplifier. The recording we know to be beautiful, but it is the link in between that we know to be wrong. To some extent we are similar to that amplifier. Way out in space there are wonderful energies coming to the Earth and through us all. We are distorting these energies to some extent, and then transmitting this distortion out again into the vast sea of all energy. If you could regard your position in life as existing within a highly-tuned mechanism, receiving energies and transmitting them out again, I feel sure that the next step to such a visualisation would be a determination on your part to still receive and transmit, but to take out the distortion factor.

Taking out the distortion factor

Taking out the 'distortion factor', to which Dr. King refers at the end of the last section, is really the journey towards enlightenment.

There is only one energy. In its purest form, it is divine. Mind patterns throughout the cosmos condition this energy for better or worse. The same energy used by a white magician to bring healing and benefit to other forms of life is the same energy used by the black magician to bring harm.

The rituals are exactly opposite in their motivation, but the energy used is the same—there is only one source. Incidentally, white and black in this context have no racial connotations whatsoever, but are only descriptive terms for the type of magic practised. All thoughts and actions are to some extent magical—whether they be white (benign), grey (mediocre) or black (harmful).

Black magic should be avoided at all costs—not only because it is harmful to others, but also because sooner or later, by Karmic Law, it always rebounds upon the practitioner, bringing him great harm. He will reap what he has sown.

We are all channels for energy all the time.

By performing spiritual practices, we can raise our consciousness to higher and higher levels, getting ever closer to the unchangeable essence of the one Source from which all energy comes. This is done by the controlled development of the major psychic centres, each of which is a seat of consciousness with its own individual characteristics.

Personal Magnetism

Channelling energy in the right way is also the key to enhancing your personal magnetism.

Personal magnetism is a dynamic expression of energy. It is a scientific attribute which can be enhanced scientifically or reduced scientifically. You can make yourself a dynamic, magnetic person, or you can lack a dynamic, magnetic personality. This is not a question of emotion, but of pure metaphysics. Magnetism is an expression, an outpouring, a radiation, a reflection of energy.

How can you enhance your magnetism? Correct breathing is one of the most important things of all. No one can breathe correctly and not be magnetic. You must be magnetic if you breathe correctly. If you practise the yoga breathing exercises you must radiate magnetism because you are taking into yourself a tremendous amount of energy, which manifests as magnetism and which gives you a more dynamic, positive and surer approach to all things. It is not possible for any man or woman to practise the breathing exercises and not be a magnetic person. It is like charging a piece of metal which has a coil on it with electricity to make it an electro-magnet. You cannot charge yourself with the universal life forces, which are carried on the air you breathe, and still remain unmagnetic.

Nearly as important is correct drinking. You have to drink sufficient liquids, especially water. This is essential to enhance your personal magnetism, more essential even than a correct diet. You can only last a few minutes without breathing before you will die. You can last for a few days without drinking and several weeks without eating. They come in that order of importance: breathing, drinking, eating. You have to have a correct, balanced diet so that the cellular structure of the body is fed correctly. You need plenty of physical exercise. The more physical exercise you have the healthier the circulation, the more improved the muscle function, the better the food is digested, and the more the aura, to a certain extent, is enabled to function correctly. If the physical body does not function correctly, then the aura will not function correctly.

The Eating Practice

The Master Aetherius:

Few of you people upon Terra are particular about where you eat. This is rather surprising considering its vital importance. You eat at any restaurant which takes your fancy, not caring whether the staff who prepared the food are contented, responsible people or not. If they are not, then the poisonous radiations of their thoughts will enter into the food which you eat and will have damaging effects upon you.

Thought is a material thing. It is a living thing. It can redeem. It can kill. It can mutate. It can love. Thought can do practically everything. But you can protect yourself against contamination by wrong thought in the following way:

Before you eat any food at all, say a little prayer over that food. Now, consciously think into being a white light from the surrounding ether. Think it into the food, so that it impregnates every molecule of mass on your plate. When it does so, you will notice (after some practice) a greyish mist coming away from the food. Now, using the first finger of the right hand, describe a circle around your plate. This action will cut away the poisonous grey mist emanating from your food so that you do not absorb it into your physical and auric bodies. The absorption of this grey misty matter would damage your aura and would also have a direct reflection upon the cellular structure of your physical body.

The practice will charge your food with vital cosmic energy, as the water practice recharges the fading energy in the liquid.

This procedure is so well explained that there is no necessity for further illustration. Those with clairvoyant faculties will be able to see the greyish mist coming away from their food after the white light has entered. Those of you who have not these powers can use such an exercise as a way to develop them.

In these days of mass catering, this practice is a must for all those people who have to eat their food in cafés and restaurants. Appreciation of the difficulties endured by the majority of us in this respect obviously prompted the giving of this practice by the Master Aetherius.

The Water Charging Practice

The Master Aetherius:

The second most important mento-physical action is that of drinking. I have been commissioned to teach you how to drink correctly. A baby knows how and what to drink, but when the baby reaches a certain age, it often drifts away from its instinctive judgement and drinks such poisons as alcohol, the result of which is loss of memory, and very strong coffee, which gives false stimulation.

The most important drink is water, the cosmic energy content of which can be easily stepped up. Now, here is a simple practice which will give to all who adopt it very great benefit.

As you know, the clouds are made up of tiny droplets of water, which are being constantly bombarded by solar energy. The town dweller, who takes his water from large storage systems, is drinking water which, through storage, has lost a great deal of its original cosmic energy. The following practice will replace that energy which will act directly upon your nervous system and stimulate your brain centres, and thereby greatly enhance your spiritual practices.

Take a dark blue bottle and fill it with cold water, after allowing the cold tap to run for a few minutes, and stand the container in the sun for 15 minutes. Then pour it into another vessel, through the air for a time or two. Drink at once with the addition of pure fruit juice if possible. The sun's rays will step up the cosmic energy charge, and pouring backwards and forwards will add an electrical charge caused by the friction of one molecule of water against its neighbour. Having studied your water supply system through our agents on Terra, we can speak with familiarity about it.

Anyone suffering from nervous debility should drink three glasses of water daily which has been recharged with cosmic energy, and within two weeks, great benefit will result.

This is a spiritual practice, because it will greatly stimulate your mental power which is one essential element of illumination. Not one of your saints was an ignorant person. It is not possible to have wisdom and ignorance at the same time.

Therapeutic Use of the Water Charging Practice

Practical applications devised by Dr. King

This practice is well known around the world. It is extremely simple, but nevertheless very beneficial to all who practise diligently.

A few spots of freshly boiled water added to the cosmic water enhances its electrical charge. This is strongly recommended for both internal and external use. Should there be no sunlight available, you can expose the blue bottle for 20 minutes under a 100 watt electric light. For external use a longer exposure is necessary.

For swollen ankles and tired, aching feet: Expose the water for six to eight hours in the sunlight or beneath a 100 watt electric light and bathe the affected parts (after washing and rinsing off all soap residue). Do not dry the cosmic water away but gently massage it in with the palms of the hands. Always massage towards the heart except when treating the spinal column, when a downward motion is recommended.

For tired, strained eyes: Bathe in lukewarm cosmic water after 15 minutes' exposure.

For a gargle and mouthwash: Use cosmic water after two hours' exposure, together with a pinch of sea salt.

For nasal catarrh or hay fever: Expose for about one hour and sniff up the nostrils morning and evening, followed by 10 to 15 minutes of deep breathing through each nostril alternately.

For baldness: Expose the water for six to eight hours and massage in briskly with the finger tips.

Most *nervous headaches* can be relieved by gently rubbing the forehead, temples and back of the neck with the water with an hour's exposure. Always allow it to dry in. Massage down the spine is very beneficial in these cases. After massaging in the first application of the water, damp the head and neck and spinal column well and allow it to dry while exposed to the air. This will make the part cool and bring relief from nervous tension. When the forehead and neck are nicely cool, gently bend the head forwards once or twice.

Bleeding from cuts: We have discovered that the charged water, after eight hours' exposure to light, assists in the relief of bleeding from cuts if applied cold directly on the cut or in the form of a wet poultice. This high charge also helps to heal the wound by promoting the growth of healthy clean tissue.

Diarrhoea: Relief will be brought about if sipped slowly after five hours' exposure.

The water, if absolutely pure in the first place, is safe to take internally after many hours of exposure to light. But it may cause a tingling on the tongue and in the throat if highly charged. This is because of its disinfectant properties, which are not harmful but very much the reverse. However, for most internal uses the exposure period of 15 minutes provides a cosmic charge of homeopathic strength which, in the majority of cases, is more beneficial than a higher charge.

The charged water will be found of great benefit if taken often during periods of either religious or health fasting. Its subtle magnetic charge, travelling as it does along the nerve sheaths, will stimulate all psychic centres in a gentle, natural way. Such a procedure will not force development, thereby causing an imbalance to the primary function of the chakras. In fact, so gentle is its action that an all-round internal harmony is brought into being which promotes a balanced stimulation and development of these important psychic centres.

It can be seen that there are dozens of ways of using this water. In fact, all water not used for hot drinks or cooking can be charged before drinking and given a vital energy which it has lost through storage in reservoirs and the travel through filter beds and piping systems.

The diligent and correct application of this knowledge can bring about the most astounding results.

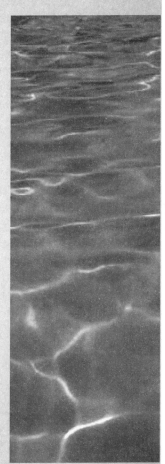

More keys to magnetism

Positive visualisation too is extremely potent. You can visualise yourself as being more magnetic than you are, more dynamic than you are, having greater power than you have got; and if you do it often enough, these visualisations will begin to manifest. In this way you can give yourself magnetic attributes.

Nothing is much good in this life unless you have spiritual ambition. All the great murderers throughout history lacked spiritual ambition, whereas all the saints had spiritual ambition. They all had a dream of some spiritual goal. If you kill off all other forms of ambition in your nature, then leave that one rose in the garden of weeds, and tend it very carefully and let it grow, because it is a beautiful flower. Without it, I believe man is little better than the animal; with it, he stands head and shoulders above other men. This is an essential attribute. It gives you drive; it gives you something to work for, a mountain to climb in your experience. It is like a magnet drawing you onwards if you keep it in your mind and allow your higher self to express itself through you in your journey towards the spiritual goal which you have set yourself. This will enhance your magnetism very much because it will tend to bring the best out of you. You have something to work for. You are not just a piece of wood drifting in the stream of life, but a young tree which is growing with purpose. A person without purpose is like a ship without a rudder—he will go nowhere except the rocks.

Striving to promote a spiritual cause and loyalty to that cause, will enhance your magnetism because you will send a message to the subconscious for help, and the subconscious will come up with many answers. You will need energy in order to work upon these answers and you will draw it to yourself. The greater the spiritual cause, the more you will answer this call. Gradually you will throw the whole of the weight of your mind and body into this call. Automatically your magnetism will be enhanced and you will be more of a radiator than ever before.

Discontentedness with world conditions is vital. The contented man is a man who has not done much for the world. If you are content with the world as it is—with people starving and dying of various diseases, with the foul atomic bomb, and all the political machinations going on, then the best thing to do is to go and play with the fairies in the woods for the rest of your life, because your life is useless anyway. I could not call the Master Jesus a contented or a happy man. He physically wept at times, until he wept tears of blood. If you can show me any true spiritual worker on any platform in the world who can honestly stand before an audience and say that at one time or another he has not wept for the world, I say that man is no good, no matter what he calls himself. You should not be discontented with everything and everybody, but discontented enough with world conditions to try to do something to put them right. This will enhance your personal magnetism, especially if you use prayer and love, which are the opposite of the strife and hate so often seen in the world.

Truthfulness is another key to personal magnetism. Somebody once asked a judge whether he would always remain truthful. Now this judge was a thinker and he said, "I would remain as truthful as I possibly could, even though I would not always tell the whole truth." There is one way to defeat untruthfulness—that is with truthfulness. You can never defeat lies with lies. If you are truthful you are fearless. Even in this world, truthfulness does have a reward and that reward is a lasting, wonderful thing. It might cost you a lot of money, but in the end, you will gain something that no money can ever buy. Truthfulness and fearlessness go hand in hand. You cannot be a dynamic magnetic being and be fearful at the same time.

All these things bring a correct balance throughout the psychic centres, which means that these floodgates in the aura are open to receive tremendous dynamic energies from the universal supply which comes from one source—the Divine. When these little floodgates are open, different types of energy surge in from the highest mind energy, right down to the more basic physical energy. You must then become a person of great light and magnetic power. You should never use your magnetic powers to control others, and whoever tells you otherwise is advocating black magic. When you have enhanced your personal magnetism you are faced with the problem of handling it correctly so that it will not harm others. It should be used only to help, raise, teach, guide and heal others. A magnetic personality can easily control a weaker personality, but that would be wrong. True personal magnetism is love in action and love is an impersonal energy.

Yoga Breathing

Of all the methods of contacting and drawing into yourself the universal life forces, yoga breathing is the most effective. Its physical benefits are well known, specifically for ailments such as asthma, bronchitis and hay fever, but also for your general well-being. By breathing from low down in the back and stomach, rather than just the chest as so many do, you will expand your lungs and thereby absorb more oxygen. A good way to test yourself is to lie on your back on a hard surface and place a fairly heavy object, such as a large book, on your midriff between your abdomen and lower ribs. As you breathe in and out, the object should rise and fall. If it does you are performing diaphragmatic breathing, which is healthy. If it does not you are practising shallow breathing from the chest only and need to change the habit by becoming aware of your ribs, lungs and diaphragm. As Dr. King said:

No shallow breather can be a deep thinker. If you breathe shallowly you can never have glorious visualisation or glorious visions. Relatively speaking, the deeper your breath, the more controlled your thoughts.

A balanced regular program of breathing exercises, such as those included in this Initiation, which are based on age-old practices, will tend to make you calmer and more able to cope with the ups and downs of life. When you are tense and stressed you will tend to breathe fast and shallowly, high up in the chest. Some chronically tense people hyperventilate—they over-breathe all the time, keeping them in a permanent state of anxiety. Hyperventilation prevents sufficient oxygen reaching the brain and can also cause migraines, dizziness, nausea and palpitations. By changing breathing habits, this can be controlled, thereby minimising tension, stress, panic and anxiety. If you do feel tensed up and uptight, such as in a traffic jam, consciously breathe out and let the tension flow away from your neck, shoulders and arms. If you are in pain, it is beneficial to breathe in to the site of the pain and let go of the pain as you breathe out, rather than trying to resist it, which tightens the muscles, restricts the flow of blood and usually makes it worse.

There are numerous other benefits from yoga breathing, including the following: increased vitality and alertness; the removal of toxins; more natural sleep; better digestion through the gentle massage of internal organs and intestines; more oxygen in the bloodstream; strengthened lungs; the control and elimination of stress; better speech and singing; and improved skin tone. There are also many mental benefits. According to yoga teaching, if the mind is moving, so are the heart and respiration. Anger and excitement cause the breath to quicken, just as sleep generally causes it to slow down. By consciously slowing down the breath and making it rhythmic, you can achieve tranquillity at will. Yoga breathing will improve concentration, memory, confidence and, certainly, psychic ability.

But the main purpose of yoga breathing, known in Sanskrit as *pranayama*, is beyond the purely physical and mental levels. It is to draw the one energy to you at an etheric level in abundance so that it can be used to enhance your spiritual development. It has been used in some form by all the great mystic schools, including the Daoists, Christians, Sufis, martial artists, as well as the yogis. The Hebrew Old Testament states in Psalm 121 Verse 6: "The sun shall not smite thee by day, nor the moon by night", which has an exact parallel in some of the Hindu Upanishads, which use the sun as a code for breathing through the right nostril and the moon as a code for breathing through the left nostril. It was believed that the pranic flow is enhanced by breathing through only one nostril at a time. At night, the flow of *prana* was such that it was best to breathe through the right nostril, and in the day, through the left nostril. Perhaps the 4th-century Father, St. Jerome, who oversaw the translation of the Old Testament into Latin, was right when he said that it was written in a code which very few fully understood.

Through deep breathing, you not only draw into your body certain gases, but you draw into the body, and through the bodies, and out again from the bodies, certain of the *pranas*, which are the universal life forces around which the whole of creation exists. Without the five minor *pranas* and the five major *pranas*, creation as we know it could not exist. Everything you see is an amalgamation of these ten energies, whether it be a glass or the water in it, or a tablecloth, or the floor, or your head, or your brain cells, or even your subtle bodies. It is an amalgamation of five major energies and five minor energies, coupled with the physical matter which these energies have drawn around themselves. So, this *prana* becomes a life force, and if it is breathed in and controlled through the bodies, then this is one sure way to develop.

A System of Yoga Breathing

The following system of yoga breathing exercises was devised by Dr. King after studying and practising *pranayama* for many years. It is a distillation of countless exercises into a safe and balanced regime which should be performed as regularly as possible. Ideally they should not be practised less than one hour before, or three hours after a meal. A perfect time is first thing in the morning, facing the rising sun. Wherever possible, at whatever time you do them, you should face the east.

The first exercise is designed to create internal harmony by breathing in and out in a measured way. This rhythmic breath will help to purify the nervous system and bring about a great feeling of peace and tranquillity never so quickly attained before. If there is catarrh present in the nasal passage, it should be removed by a nasal douche of a mild solution of salt and warm water, followed by an eye bath of charged water at blood heat.

The First Breathing

Step 1

Sit upright, with chest, neck and head held in a straight line. It is preferable to sit on the floor, tailor-fashion or other suitable yoga sitting posture, for all these exercises, but should this prove to be uncomfortable, a straight-backed wooden chair will suffice.

Do not hunch up your shoulders. Keep the spine straight and the rest of the body relaxed at the same time.

Step 2

Now, breathe in slowly and steadily through both nostrils for a count which is within your capacity.

Step 3

Next, breathe out for the same count, thereby making the inhalation the same length as the exhalation.

Pull in the diaphragm lightly upon exhalation to squeeze gently as much air as possible from the lungs.

Step 4

After a little practice, the in- and out-breaths will automatically equal each other. When this stage has been reached, you can then add the mental affirmation, which should flow in and out without any strain of any kind.

I AM NOW PURIFYING MY MIND AND BODY.

Careful practice of this exercise for at least 15 minutes daily for the first two weeks, will prepare you for the next exercise, which is a little more advanced.

The Second Breathing

Step 1

Sit straight, as before. Bend the first and second fingers of the right hand inward and lock them in position just behind the thumb. The third and fourth fingers should be extended straight outwards on one side of the clenched fingers, and the thumb also extended outwards (see illustration). This is a useful finger position because the left nostril can be closed by slight pressure from the two fingers which are extended and the right nostril can be closed by slight pressure from the thumb. Later on, both nostrils can be closed at the same time by using the fingers and thumb. This hand sign can be performed equally well by either hand, and has a very deep occult significance.

Step 2

Stop up the left nostril and breathe in through the right nostril for a measured count, according to your own capacity.

Step 3

Then close both nostrils and retain the breath for twice as long as you took to inhale.

Step 4

Now exhale through the left nostril for the same count as before, then, without pause, inhale through the left nostril again and retain as before. Then exhale through the right nostril and repeat.

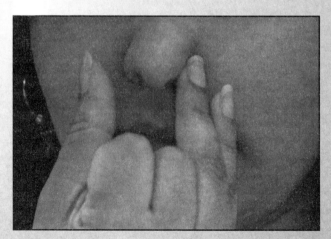

This makes one complete round of the breathing. For example, if you took 6 counts to inhale through the right nostril, then retain the breath for 12 counts. Exhale through the left for 6 counts; inhale through the left again for 6 counts, retain for 12 counts and exhale through the right for 6 counts.

You may start by performing three complete rounds and gradually increase the length of breath and retention, and the number of rounds when you are able.

Try to count automatically on your fingers during this exercise by sliding your thumb over your other fingers and counting each finger joint in turn.

Important Note
Make sure your head does not lean forward on your shoulders and tighten up during this breathing. This is the usual tendency with most beginners who are concentrating very hard upon the actual breath itself. Once in a while think of your posture and keep your shoulders relaxed with neck and spine straight. Do not strain yourself in any way.

Please remember, the count for inhalation, retention and exhalation in all these exercises is a matter to be decided by you—and you alone. A good teacher will give you a rhythm only and never a length of breath, because your life span can be lengthened by the depth of your breathings and consequently shortened by the shallowness of them. This applies to every living being who is in the first stages of adeptship.

When you have completely mastered the timing of this breathing and are able to make the counts on your fingers without thinking about them, you can use the following great spiritual affirmation while holding your breath. Do this mentally and concentrate upon its meaning with great reverence and to the exclusion of all other thoughts:

I AM NOW FILLING MY MIND AND BODY WITH THE MIGHTY POWER OF GOD.

The Third Breathing

This is similar to the last one, but instead of the breath being retained in the lungs, you now hold it outside, following the same rhythmic pattern as before, i.e. inhale through the right nostril and exhale at once through the left nostril, holding the lungs empty for twice as long as the inhalation.

Then breathe in through the left nostril and breathe out through the right nostril, and hold the breath outside of the lungs.

This breathing is easier than the last one, but you should take the same precautions as before, namely, guarding against tension in the shoulders and the head coming forward.

Important Note

Do not hold out the breath so long that you gasp upon the inhalation. Use common sense and be guided by your own knowledge of your capacity.

According to experts on the subject, this breathing is not in any way dangerous but rather brings great benefit.

Practise for three complete rounds at first, immediately following the second exercise, and increase the number of rounds of both exercises evenly.

Use the same great affirmation of power as before, but of course, this time when the breath is held out of the body:

I AM NOW FILLING MY MIND AND BODY WITH THE MIGHTY POWER OF GOD.

Notes on the Second and Third Breathings

Keep a balance between them

The Second and Third Breathings are designed to provide a perfect balance for each other. They should be done to the same count.

Holding the breath out of the body

There is an ancient saying that 'nature abhors a vacuum'. In other words, where there is a void, there is a natural tendency for it to be filled. This principle lies behind the Third Breathing. In this exercise the breath, and therefore *prana* is emptied from the body and this state of emptiness is maintained for twice the count used to breathe in and out. This creates a need for the body and aura to be filled with prana.

Since *prana* is not being taken in through the lungs, it will try to find another way in, and the only route is directly through the psychic centres. Consequently the Third Breathing is an extremely powerful way to activate the psychic centres and prepare you for the powerful exercises that are to follow.

The affirmation

The affirmation given by Dr. King for use while holding the breath is very powerful indeed and attention should be paid to doing it as well as possible. Naturally the same applies to the affirmations used with the other exercises.

Repeat it silently—you cannot repeat it any other way while holding the breath. Just *think* it if you like. Fast, definite, quite dynamically and with great surety—not a sloppy repetition, but a dynamic repetition, a sure repetition.

Give it some power—it is far better to repeat it once correctly than two or three times incorrectly. Remember that and really try to concentrate on it.

The Fourth Breathing

This exercise is almost unequalled in its effect upon brain stimulation and bodily purification. When practised properly by the adept, the most outstanding results can be brought about, but the western beginner should proceed cautiously and not miss any of the preliminary stages as laid down here.

Step 1

Sit as before and breathe in deeply through both nostrils equally.

Step 2

Then throw the breath out quickly through both nostrils and inhale again without pause. Upon exhalation, pull in the diaphragm completely to empty the lungs.

Step 3

Keep up this bellow-like action for five inhalations, then retain the breath for as long as possible without imposing any strain whatever upon yourself.

While retaining the breath, close the eyes and concentrate upon a spot between the eyebrows and about six inches in front of the forehead.

At first you will see nothing; then you will see vague moving lights. When you see a really bright light, which seems to be radiating from your forehead outwards, you may know that you are really making rapid strides.

At first it will not appear to be too easy for you to concentrate on a spot in space, about six inches in front of the forehead, and concentrate on an affirmation at the same time. It should be remembered that such mental exercises are an essential part of a course of yoga. First of all, as with all affirmations, learn them by heart so that the repetition can be performed with belief and deep feeling, demanding only part of your concentration. When this technique has been mastered, then you should have no problem to repeat an affirmation with a part of the consciousness and concentrate on the reflected light from the psychic centre in the aura of the head, approximately six inches in front of the forehead.

Do not concentrate on the physical forehead itself—the physical spot between the eyebrows—as such a practice is dangerous without the personal guidance and physical presence of a master.

Use the following affirmation of mastery while retaining the breath:

I AM DIVINE SPIRIT. I AM NOW MASTERING MY MIND AND BODY.

Important Note
While performing this exercise, guard against any build-up of muscular tension in the shoulders or neck muscles. Only the diaphragm should move in and out and the chest should rise and fall with each breath. The head and shoulders should be held straight, yet as relaxed as possible.

Perform this exercise three times. Only after regular practice for a week or two should you increase the number of breaths gradually, one by one, before retention, in keeping with your individual capacity.

The Fifth Breathing

This is the last actual breathing exercise in the present course. If each one is practised in chronological order as laid down, they will combine to form a complete course of breathings, each one performing its allotted task and dovetailing perfectly into the next to form a whole.

Step 1
Sit upright as before. Open your lips very slightly. Close the teeth and place the tip of your tongue gently behind the joining sets of teeth.

Step 2
Now, inhale slowly, causing a hissing noise where the tongue and teeth meet.

Step 3
Exhale slowly and silently through both nostrils. Repeat in the same way.

On the in-breath, try to visualise the *prana* actually entering the tip of your tongue and travelling to the base of the spinal column. On the out-breath, imagine you are bringing the vibrant pranic energy from the base of the spine straight up through the centre of the spinal column to the Christ Centre, which is situated between the eyebrows and a few inches in front of the forehead. Meditation upon the actual spot between the eyebrows can be dangerous without careful guidance but not if the attention is moved to the correct spot in space.

Practise this breathing for three times at first, and increase slowly and steadily, depending upon your ability to do so without the imposition of any strain.

Important Note

If you moisten the tongue first, the droplets of water on the very tip will vibrate quickly, causing a sipping noise. This is what is required because the vibration will promote the excretion of a rare glandular fluid which will emanate from the tip of the tongue. Once you have tasted this fluid, you will want more, for whatever your tastes, this will be the most exquisite of all. The finest French sweetmeats cannot compare with it, because this is the mystical nectar often referred to by Greek and Hindu philosophers alike. This fluid excretion will help to promote harmony and radiate health to the mental and physical structure of the student.

Use the wonderful affirmation of the Great White Brotherhood while performing this breathing, just at the end of the exhalation:

I AM ONE WITH THE LIGHT OF GOD WHICH NEVER FAILS.

The Sixth Breathing

Although the breath is held during this exercise, it is not usually classed as a breathing exercise. In fact, it is perhaps the greatest spiritual exercise known to man, for continued, careful practice—after the other breathings—will lead towards meditation, the illumination of the soul by the spirit.

In the ancient book of *I-Ching*, which was the manual of the Chinese adepts, it says that those who perform this practice, dismissing all sense objects, progress a thousand years for every time they do it.

Step 1

Sit upright as before. Take as deep a breath as possible through both nostrils.

Then stop up your ears with the thumbs, the eyes with the first fingers, the nose with the second fingers and the mouth with the remaining fingers.

Step 2

Retain the breath as long as possible.

Important Note

To gain maximum benefits, you should gently press your eyes inward and gaze upwards towards the spot between the eyebrows.

When you do this, you see a light "in the head", as it were. Concentrate upon that light to the exclusion of all else.

If you do not see any light, then you will hear a drumming noise in your ears. Concentrate upon that noise to the exclusion of all else.

As can be seen from these instructions, the student must make his own choice of concentration points: the light or the sound. If both are used alternately, progress will be slower but wonderfully balanced.

The conscious mind will gradually become aware of the wondrous beauty of the Christ Centre (the light), and the Heart Centre (the sound), and great mental and spiritual expansion will result.

Perform this exercise once only at the end of the breathings. Expel your breath when necessary, sit in a straight but comfortable posture and continue concentration upon the chosen phenomena for as long as possible.

When you are ready, great enlightenment will come; an answer to all your problems will be revealed in such a way that you will become your own teacher, the student of your higher self.

You send out power and more power still comes back.

You send out more power still and even more power still comes back!

Dr. George King

The Fifth Initiation
Radiating Spiritual Powers

Dynamic Prayer

In essence, prayer is simply the radiating of spiritual powers through the person who prays to the object of the prayer. The more intensity behind the prayer, the more dynamic, and hence effective, it will be.

According to the dictionary, prayer is: "A solemn request to God or object of worship." There are several kinds of prayer as we all know. There is a personal type of prayer for oneself; there is a personal type of prayer for another; there is an impersonal type of prayer for mankind. A good illustration of what I term as an impersonal type of prayer is included in The Twelve Blessings. Each of these prayers can be said in many different ways. They can be said as the orthodox church would have them said—without feeling, without

Through dynamic prayer we can radiate power through ourselves to the object of our prayer.

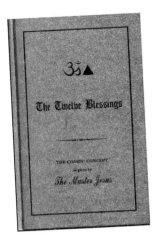

Dr. George King channelled the Master Jesus, who delivered the revolutionary system of prayer known as The Twelve Blessings.

When we perform this wonderful practice we send energy out to entities and group-souls greater than ourselves, and even to the Wondrous Absolute Itself.

The stream of energy we receive in return then allows us to send out even more energy, and to raise our consciousness in the process.

effort, without energy, without belief. Or they can be said correctly, in a dynamic fashion.

The main difference between ordinary prayer and dynamic prayer is the depth of expression. One is a shallow appeal, as though you were asking the grocer for two pounds of apples; and the other a deep expression of your inner feeling—a belief in yourself that you are capable of praying in this way and that this is the way which will bring results. If ordinary prayer is an expression of a very small portion of the conscious mind of man, then dynamic prayer must surely be a spiritual song coming from deep within. And to sing this song with your soul you must use effort, power, will, love, concentration and direction.

People are limited by themselves. All you have to do is look around you to discover that under certain predetermined conditions, the robot in which you live—called the human body—has tremendous capabilities. There are reported cases of men lifting rocks off other men or themselves which normally would take five men to lift. We have in The Aetherius Society, members who are capable of concentration to such an extent that unusual performance has been achieved by them because of their concentration, determination and inner knowledge that they can do it. Dynamic prayer is an example of this.

Dynamic prayer definitely requires a greater effort than prayer said in the normal half-hearted fashion. If ordinary prayer is a lifeless appeal to Divinity, then dynamic prayer is a deep expression of soul-feeling put behind that appeal. It is because of the effort expended in dynamic prayer that truly great results are brought about by its use. If you cast your bread upon the waters, it is said, this will return after many days. In other words, in order to bring about a result, you must expend the effort to guarantee that this result is brought about, whether or not that result is feeding yourself or praying for another who is sick.

I believe that most people—not all in this life—but most people, are capable of a form of dynamic prayer if only they will expend sufficient effort; if only they will rise above the lazy habits which they have brought upon themselves throughout the years. Such people may be fine workers; they may be people you can trust in the business world to do whatever job they say they will do correctly. Yet, when it

If ordinary prayer is an expression of a very small portion of the conscious mind of man, then dynamic prayer must surely be a spiritual song coming from deep within.

A Preparatory Practice

A mystic visualisation to invoke energies

Before commencing prayer, mantra or healing, the following colour visualisation exercise is very beneficial. This can be done either seated on a hard-backed chair or standing up.

Visualise a pink flame, which is associated with love, coming down from above the head; down the back of the head, neck and spine; then curl it under the spine and take it up the front of the body opposite the spine, to the top of the head. Imagine it going over the head and repeat the visualisation until you have two pink bands of light encircling the upper part of the body. Then detach from this completely and perform the aura cleansing practice (see page 47) until the violet flame has travelled up, through and above you. Then visualise a white light coming down through the whole of the head, neck and shoulders into the heart centre in the aura and outwards to the world.

You are then ready to begin channelling spiritual powers.

comes to prayer, they have convinced themselves that they are not capable of saying it in a dynamic fashion, and they take a lot of convincing.

Dynamic prayer is not so much the result of training as it is the result of an unshakable belief in God and a burning desire to help another or mankind. Those people who say that they are incapable of dynamic prayer are really saying that they are not spiritual enough to really want to help others. If you really want to help others you will find the way and the means to do so. When you have been shown that way and have created those means, then it is up to you to use those means in that way.

One of the most mild-mannered, soft-spoken men I know is one of the most dynamic prayers. If you knew him as I do, you would see the tremendous difference: it is as though he allows the great powers within him to take control of him—and he manifests the spiritual powers. He does not run into uncontrolled emotionalism; his prayers are expressions of pure concentration and the very essence of the person comes forward. He is not the only one who does this. There is nothing wrong with being gentle—even because of your gentleness, you can bring about a greater change within yourself at certain times, not in spite of it. Just think about that for a while.

If you really have a burning desire to help others there is one sure way that you can help others; that is with the use of dynamic prayer. Everybody can pray. There are hundreds of different prayers written so that you can use whichever prayer you choose, whichever prayer you feel you should use. As far as The Aetherius Society is concerned, we would recommend the prayers from The Twelve Blessings and those from our *Book of Sacred Prayers*, but there are thousands of others on Earth to choose from.

If people say, "Oh, I am not capable of dynamic prayer," go and hurt them and they will prove that they are capable of a dynamic scream! If you had seen the horrors which unfortunately I saw during the bombing of England in the last war, you would soon be convinced that people can scream in the most dynamic way if they are hurt badly enough. Those same people may not have believed they were capable of dynamic prayer though.

This information can change your life; it can make you into a more useful person than you have been in the past, and when it does, then your practice and expenditure of effort will have been worthwhile. When you pray to God, never give of your second best, and that is what most people are doing. If they would give of their best, then dynamic prayer would flow through them. But they have got to give of their best all the time they are praying in order to allow this to happen.

I believe that most people are capable of dynamic prayer to one degree or another. The question is, though, are they willing to expend sufficient effort to perform dynamic prayer—not whether they can pray dynamically. That is the question to ask yourself and the answer should be in the affirmative. It is not easy; it demands concentration, it demands belief, it demands deep respect for God, it demands inner knowledge, but above all these—except the respect for God—it demands a burning desire to bring about certain predetermined results. If you have this, it does not matter who you are, you can pray in not only a dynamic fashion, but in the most effective fashion. Your output, from an energy point of view, is approaching the stage of the adept.

Dynamic prayer is one sure way of manipulating your karma in a very helpful fashion on your own behalf, especially if it is used for mass healing of the human race. There can be no higher motive than this for your prayer, certainly not on this Earth. But you have to have the will to do it; you have to have a burning desire to do it; you have to be spiritual enough and sensitive enough to feel for others. If you cannot feel for others then you are not a spiritual person! All people are capable of having feelings for others. Allow this inner power to manifest. It will never manifest until you allow it to do so—until you, the controller, orders: "You will now manifest!"

Dynamic prayer is a wonderful expression. It is a song of the soul and the soul wants to sing; it wants to express light all around itself; it wants to go forward and help and raise others who need the transmuting power output of a joyous soul. You must allow your inner soul to do this; you must allow this beautiful manifestation to take place, this great surge of energy to fill your mind and aura to such an extent that the bread you cast upon the waters is indeed plentiful and beneficial to all. And the more effort you expend in this respect, the more sure the result must be. This is the Law. If you want an impossible thing it is

this: you cannot send out dynamic prayers for mankind without having certain results. It is impossible, it cannot be done. The results must come sooner or later. If all the billions of people on this planet prayed dynamically one morning, before the afternoon the world would be changed completely!

Do not be deluded by your lower selves, or even by that allegedly logical part of yourself, which is sometimes the most illogical part of all—your conscious mind, but do let your soul sing. It can be taken over by the higher part of you, and the change will amaze you. Once you have mentally tasted this, you will not want to slip back again.

Some of the greatest prayers in this world were undoubtedly the ancient Sufis. They used to pray for about four days and four nights—and very fervently indeed. In fact, so fervently, that they were on the verge of madness. But they controlled themselves in such a way that they were able to precipitate deep meditative conditions. This is one of the results of dynamic prayer. Ordinary people may not pray for four days and nights, but they can pray with enthusiasm. This is the difference between success and failure in many cases.

The first rule to observe in dynamic prayer is enthusiasm. Without this, you cannot hope to pray correctly in a dynamic fashion. If you lack enthusiasm, try to cultivate it. If you do not put enthusiasm into prayer, you are only paying lip service. You are only saying so many words. We have all heard lip service prayer in orthodox establishments—words just repeated with no feeling, without any enthusiasm. These people might just as well have said words like, "cat, dog, cat, dog" for their prayers have meant only that.

If you have a deep feeling for humanity, and if you allow this deep feeling, that innate kindness, to come to the surface, then you will pray with great feeling. This is the secret of it. It is not what you say, or how long you say it, but what you mean when you say it that counts. If, on the other hand, you allow yourself to get into a sleepy, negative type of condition, almost bordering on negative trance, you are hindering yourself as a channel. You are just like a piece of blotting paper soaking up energy.

Two major forms of energy can be released during prayer. One, a slow, beautiful energy of love; the other, a dynamic, powerful, tremendous energy. I am not

Dynamic prayer is a wonderful expression. It is a song of the soul and the soul wants to sing.

going to say which is best—they both have many things to recommend them. I would say that, especially in these days, the latter type is needed. Dynamic prayer is the secret to have at this time in world history. It is a way of releasing tremendous energy. With this, of course, goes absolute and strict control over your emotions. Do not let your emotions rule you, but transmute these emotions into a spiritual energy. Dynamic prayer is one sure way of doing this.

Dynamic prayer develops a most colourful personality; it brings out something within you, if it is put to spiritual purpose. The more dynamic prayer you perform, the less temper you will find you will have because you have burned up certain facets of your emotion by transmuting them into spiritual channels. Your temper will automatically become more balanced. If you are a person who might be considered as dull and uncolourful, you will soon bring colour to your everyday life; you will soon be charged with a tremendous power.

When you start dynamic prayer you will get reactions in your own psychological make-up, depending upon the amount of success you have. If you are a mild, gentle person, you will still get reactions. If you are a dynamic person, the reaction may not seem to be as great, yet it will manifest. There will come times when you will be right at the top of the mountain, and others when you will be right in the depths of the valley. I am afraid that this is one of the things you will have to suffer until you are strong enough to be able to rise above these things. Please try to remember, though, the tops of the mountains at those times you are in the depths. You will have experiences of a mystic nature which will mean a tremendous amount to you. You will see visions. Please do not relate them to anyone else. Do not even become attached to them, save to be of assistance to you when you hit bottom, as you will. If any person tells me that they have prayed in a dynamic fashion yet have not experienced depression, I will not believe those people, no matter who they are.

There will also be another reaction taking place, very gradually, in a balanced way within you. You may not even notice it— that is a definite advancement. As you go on in this way, the visions you will get will sometimes become so clear as to be startling. Do not attach yourself to them. Note them, give thanks if you want, but then detach. As these occur, certain other aspects of you, of a deeper spiritual nature, will gradually grow very strongly. A change will come over you. You will become as a strong tree in a breeze. You will slowly and surely begin to kill fear. Nobody can be dynamic and fearful at the same time. The people who are fearful are generally the negative type of people. Be positive and dynamic. You will then know real faith, and advance. All this, and more, is a result of prayer.

I can remember praying so dynamically once that I flew round the room. I was physically weightless under another, higher system of laws. During another session of dynamic prayer, I saw through walls and all physical objects. In fact, two people were giving healing in the same room and I could see, not only the two auric bodies of these people, but also their skeletons. Dynamic prayer can bring a rise of *kundalini*. There are other ways of course to raise *kundalini*, but dynamic prayer is one of them, because it is an important aspect of service to others.

The Prayer Mudra

a powerful position for radiating spiritual powers

Stand with the hands raised and visualise white light radiating outwards from the heart centre and the palms of the hands to the object of your prayer.

How to Pray

Prayer is a way to direct energy by thought with love. If you imagined, when you were praying, a small chariot was going away from yourselves, the chariot would be love and the load that it was carrying would be the universal life force, or *prana*. *Prana* is given out by the sun and every 32 minutes exactly, it changes from one *prana* to another one. Every one of the five main *pranas* are, of course, extremely beneficial and necessary, not only to your life, but to the life of the person you were praying for, and the world as a whole. You send out a stream of pranic energy with love.

The more you can control your thoughts, the better you can pray; and the better you pray, the surer will be the result. Prayer is an act of magic which, if done correctly, will produce so-called miraculous results. It depends upon your state of concentration. I would say, start learning to pray by taking up some kind of concentrative practice. Nobody is capable of very effective prayer unless their breathing is fairly well controlled and balanced. Before you start to pray, charge yourself with some breathing exercises, and while you are praying, try to keep the breath in control. You must be able to draw the energy into yourself so that you can send it out and once you begin to send it out successfully, it will then flow through you and you become a channel.

The Sufis used to have a ritualistic prayer as one of their main ways of going into meditation. They would start by reciting mantras, which is the highest form of prayer, and they would gradually go on praying in an inspirational way. The prayers were not written for them, but they would allow the inspiration to flow until they became nearly mad; and then they would stop, control all the energies perfectly, and go into deep meditation for as long as they chose. By the recitation of mantra in the correct manner, they would cause their aura to move at very high velocities. Instead of the aura being static, it would begin to move around them and it would go on moving around them until it reached quite a considerable velocity. Then they would be inside a huge magnetic field and tremendous energies were invoked. If you have anything static, and rotate anything around it very fast, that static thing must become charged with tremendous energies caused by the rotation around it. They would rotate their

The Secret of Dynamic Prayer

How to radiate power for healing and inspiration to others

The way to pray is to direct the power from the palms of the hands and from the heart centre. Now, in that position, which I call the prayer mudra, you are free—nothing is locked; energy comes down through you and outward. You are virtually giving all to the target or recipient of your prayer. You are directing the prayer outward and leaving all the centres free so that power can go out.

Prayer, if you want to make it work, must come from your very heart and soul—you must put your very life's blood into it, if it is to work. Your personalities must be sunk and you must give way to a deep feeling of love for all. You can pray for half an hour and you can release "x" units of energy. You can pray for two minutes and you can release "x" units of energy. It is up to you. I would strongly advise people in the beginning to make it fast, because the greatest energies flow immediately. Train yourself to get this energy at once and you will always be able to do it. The first word will bring virtual sparks of energy from you.

After you have said your prayer, which might be for your friend's health, your own health, for the health of the world as a whole, for world peace—finish by giving thanks to whatever higher Source you choose to give thanks to. Send out your thanks, because you have sent energy outward and that, to you, has been a great privilege. It should be considered a privilege to be used as a channel for energy. By giving thanks in the right way you have done something far more important than thanks, you have set a seal on your prayer. You have put the last full stop in, because your thanks have said, "I have faith in the fact that this prayer will work."

The Sealing Mudra

The correct way to close your prayer and healing sessions

After you have finished praying, I will give you a Tibetan mudra to use. It is practised by the highest initiates and adepts in Tibet and also in many mystic schools throughout the world. After you finish praying, simply brush the palms of both hands together. Brush the right palm over the left, keeping the left hand flat and pointing away from you. Then with the right hand, fingers pointing to the left, brush away from you and say: "It is done." The very action of doing this cuts off the energy which has flowed through you and signifies your detachment from what you have done. This sealing mudra can be used after prayer and healing.

The right hand palm is rubbed across the left hand palm to signify the completion of channelling spiritual powers through prayer, mantra or healing.

You can say mentally or aloud:
It is done
or
Thy will, oh Mighty God, be done

aura around themselves, become highly charged and then send out this high charge. Some of their prayers must have made Shakespeare look like a child; they must have been some of the most magnificent prose ever uttered on Earth.

After completing a prayer session or an individual prayer during which you have used the prayer mudra, it is advisable to use the sealing mudra. This is done by passing the palms of the hands across each other, as though you were wiping something away. This both seals the psychic centres in the palms which have been activated during your prayers, and symbolically ends the ritual you have just performed. In turn, this brings about an essential detachment from the prayer, which is one of the secrets of its success. Having prayed for a certain cause, you need to allow the magic to work by not focusing on it afterwards.

Choosing a Prayer

It is vital to choose a prayer which is worded correctly, such as the one overleaf, delivered by the Master Jesus through Dr. King on December 20th, 1961.

To help in identifying a correctly worded prayer, Dr. King made the following brilliant analysis of the Lord's Prayer and the New Lord's Prayer.

The Lord's Prayer

"Our Father which art in Heaven" — This I maintain to be a mistake. God cannot be in heaven or anywhere else because It is in all places at one and the same time; therefore, to limit It at all is a mistake. If it said "Our Father", if you want to call Him that, "which art in all places", it would be more correct. The word "which" is good because it implies that God is sexless.

"Hallowed be Thy Name" — The different names of God are, of course, in all ways hallowed. They are very sacred and should always be treated as such. Throughout history we have been given different names for God, or for a part of God. It does not say here what name they are hallowing. It was possibly a Sanskrit term, but when the Bible was rewritten, a lot of Sanskrit terms were left out.

"Thy kingdom come" — This is a prophecy and a good one. The heaven as seen coming to Earth by the visionaries and prophets throughout the centuries is going to come. But this prayer is extremely limited in its boundaries, probably so that it could be understood easily by limited thinkers and fit in better with the orthodox dogma which was being created.

"Thy Will be done" — The Will of God, or the Law of Karma, must come about. There is not any force that is greater than this. Contrary to all appearances, this will be done. In this respect, the prayer is a good one.

"On Earth, as it is in Heaven" — This is orthodoxy creeping in, but it really means that the great evolution, as enjoyed in certain spheres, will also be enjoyed on the basic physical plane in time.

"Give us this day our daily bread" — This is a very unfortunate way of making an appeal that we may be inspired in such a manner that our daily needs are met because of this inspiration. I feel that is what is meant, though it is poorly expressed.

The New Lord's Prayer

Oh Divine and Wondrous Spirit!
Oh Everlasting Lord of Hosts!
Send forth, now, through me,
Thy great and lasting Power.

Allow me, oh Mighty God, the lasting privilege
Of radiating to all the world, Thy great Love,
So that those who suffer may be given the
Power and energy to rise above their weaknesses.

Oh Mighty God, in great humility do I ask You
To send forth Your Power,
To give to me this great lasting privilege
Of being a channel, so that my suffering brothers
May be helped and guided and healed and
Lifted into Thy Light;
So that they who know not, may look up,
And in doing so, receive through their Higher Selves,
your Divine Counsel.

Oh Mighty God, this day have You granted me
A Divine privilege.
I ask You, now, to give to me the strength,
So that never again will I turn from my inner vision of You.
Om Shanti Shanti Shanti.

In praise of Your Greatness, oh God,
Doth my Soul sing.
Grant it energy to sing on
Forever and forever.

"And forgive us our trespasses" — Jesus was a practical metaphysician who, many, many times, demonstrated his powers. I do not believe that he would make a statement like this because it is wrong. An advanced avatar would not intimate for one moment that any of us can be forgiven our trespasses for those things we do wrong.

This line is conditioned by the next line which says, "As we forgive those who trespass against us." When you put both lines together, it is not so bad. There is an intimation here that karma does exist; that as we do unto others, so others can be expected to do unto us—but I think it is too veiled. I think it has been cleverly written so that it is veiled because, you know, the big danger to orthodoxy was to talk about karma, as then you must talk about reincarnation. And when you talk about reincarnation, you have an entirely different religion. I think it would have been a lot better had it appeared like this: "As we forgive those who trespass against us, we are forgiven our trespasses." This is exactly how the Law of Karma does work and this would then make some sense.

"And lead us not into temptation" — There is a strong intimation here that God would lead us into temptation, which, of course, is absolutely ridiculous.

"But deliver us from evil" — This is an intimation that unless we ask God to deliver us from evil, we will not be delivered from evil. God is depicted as a cruel, but nevertheless wise, individual, who will want to deliver us to any evil or hell, unless we confess and ask not to be delivered to these places. This is wrong.

"For Thine is the kingdom, the power and the glory" — This is true because there is only one power, one glory, and that is the power that comes from The Absolute and the glory which will go back to It.

"Forever and Forever" — The "forever and forever" is excellent.

So the Lord's Prayer in that version will not withstand any real examination in the light of a degree of metaphysical knowledge.

The New Lord's Prayer

"Oh Divine and Wondrous Spirit" — This is an intimation that God is not a Father living in heaven, but an all-pervasive Force—or if you like, an Essence or Spirit.

"Oh Everlasting Lord of Hosts" — An intimation here that there are other Gods— other great Beings, but there is One Absolute, Creative Source from which these other great Beings came.

"Send forth, now, through me, Thy great and lasting Power" — From the centre of all things, must come the Power. No matter who it comes through, it must come from the One Source, or The Absolute. So, those first four sentences begin to put God, or The Absolute, in something like Its rightful place.

"Allow me, oh Mighty God, the lasting privilege of radiating to all the world, Thy great Love" — Here you are obeying certain laws: as I send out, so shall I receive; I am my brother's keeper; I am one with all the universe. You are saying: allow me to send out power and energy. I admit that being used as a channel for Your great love, which I am now tuning myself into, is a lasting privilege.

"So that those who suffer may be given the power and energy to rise above their weaknesses" — All suffering, unless the suffering is suffered by an avatar like Jesus, is a result of weakness, because of something they have done wrong, either in this life or a previous life. Suffering is one of the finest teachings. It is certainly not the only teacher. Man does not have to suffer—he chooses to suffer. To ask that people might "be given the power and energy to overcome their weaknesses" is to transmute their karma; to rise above their sickness, illness, starvation; to translate it entirely onto another plane; to do away with it completely.

"Oh Mighty God, in great humility do I ask You to send forth Your Power; to give to me this great lasting privilege of being a channel, so that my suffering brothers may be helped and guided and healed and lifted into Thy Light" — This is a repetition of the same plea in a different manner. "Of being a channel" is an admission, a belief and a faith that if we go about things in the right way, we can become a channel for this Love—and we can. "Helped and guided" admits that it is possible for this power to come down to guide a person. People may not know where their guidance comes from. It might come through you. They do not know, neither, probably, do you. That is why it is so essential to say prayers like this over and over again. You do not know just what good you may be doing. "And healed" — This is a belief in healing. "I can heal" is the correct intimation.

"So that they who know not may look up, and in doing so, receive through their Higher Selves, Your Divine Counsel" — In other words, they look within and raise their consciousness up. It is happening every second of every hour of every day of every year, somewhere in the world. They look within, great elation fills them, and they begin to realise that there is something more in life than their narrow environment. You, living on the other side of the world, may have been the channel through which this spark was ignited. "Your Divine Counsel" means that through their elation they are inspired. Perhaps it is the first time they have ever thought seriously about God.

"Oh Mighty God, this day have you granted me a Divine privilege" — In other words, I am greatly privileged to be used as a channel for your wonderful power, which I have full faith in because it has passed through me.

"I ask You, now, to give to me the strength" — First of all, I have asked to be used as a channel to heal all who need to be healed and, after that, I ask for myself.

"So that never again will I turn from my inner vision of You" — If we are to enjoy always our inner vision of even our limited

May Your Light Shine

A prayer for power radiation

Oh Divine and Wondrous God,
We pray that Your Light may shine
*   upon us—NOW,*
So that we may be lifted up,
So that we may be made strong,
So that we may stand as sentinels
Radiating Thy Light unto all the world;
So that man might see this Light,
And be guided by it.

Oh Mighty God,
Give us the ability to allow
The Power from Thy Heart
To flow through us;
That we might forever be as
A lighthouse to men,
Radiating hope, power, healing,
Love and inspiration to all.

The Master Jesus

Prayer for Spiritual Workers

A prayer for protection and strength

*O*h Mighty God, I Bless all those
Who, because of their limitations,
Would smite me.

Oh Mighty God, I Bless all those
Who, because of their weakness,
Would not heed me.

Oh Mighty God, I Bless all those
Who, because of their ignorance,
Would defile You, through me.

And I ask, oh Mighty God, oh Wondrous Power,
That Your Strength may be given to me now;
So that I might be fortified by this,
So that I might go forward bravely into the world,
And despite reception, send forth my Love of Thee,
Throughout all races of man.

Oh Mighty God, give me the power and strength
To rise above my Karmic weakness,
The deficiencies in the pattern of my evolution,
So that I might evolve and become stronger,
Aye, and even stronger, in Thy Everlasting Light,
Oh God, Thy Will be done.

The Master Jesus

concept of God, we would do so in meditation. Some of us are forced to turn away from that in order to serve humanity. However, we can still ask for the strength so that any time we may allow ourselves to enjoy this inner vision.

"Om Shanti Shanti Shanti" — This is a sacred Sanskrit mantra which cannot be fully translated. A very literal translation would be: "I am great peace, great peace, great peace."

"In praise of Your greatness, oh God" — Your greatness, Your all-expansive, all-inclusive greatness.

"Doth my soul sing" — Not my brain, but my soul.

"Grant it energy to sing on forever and forever" — The Spirit has the energy to sing on forever and forever, because it is the direct link with the higher form of The Absolute. But the soul is a much lower link, which manifests as high intelligence. Just as your aura is absolutely and completely physical on a certain level, so is the soul completely physical, even though it be an energy essence. So it needs the strength to sing on forever and forever. Where will it get that strength from? From the spirit which is the Source. That is the

deep implication of this final statement. This is a superb, perfectly balanced prayer from a metaphysical point of view.

Ecclesiastical Mysticism

Understandably, people associate the ecclesiastical tradition of the Christian church with orthodoxy. Yet behind it lies a powerful mysticism. The purpose of the ordination of ministers and priests and the consecration of bishops, was to enhance the flow of spiritual powers through the individual. There is absolutely no reason why this should be restricted to men—on the contrary, a balance between male and female energies is preferable wherever possible in conducting spiritual rituals.

The principle behind ordination and consecration is called in the church the "apostolic succession". It is believed that the power originating with Jesus and passed through St. Peter can be channelled through successive generations of bishops, providing the link from one to another remains unbroken. This principle is also followed in eastern systems of initiation, where the guru-disciple chain of initiation is regarded as crucial. Certain Tibetan lamas also followed this mystical law of succession. It is, in fact, far more powerful and reliable than the hereditary principle of royal and noble houses, which relies purely on physical blood lines and genetic inheritance. Blood may be thicker than water, but a spiritual heritage is far more potent from both a mystical and karmic point of view.

Many of the rituals used by orthodox religions have their roots in mystical procedures, though they have often lost or modified the power of the original practice. The theosophist and bishop in the Liberal Catholic Church, C.W. Leadbeater, observed clairvoyantly the power of rituals such as the eucharist, as well as the fact that ecclesiastical vestments, such as the stole, biretta and chasuble, channel spiritual energies in different ways.

Mantra Yoga

Although western religious rituals have a great mystical power when performed correctly, the most effective method of invoking spiritual energy is the practice of Mantra Yoga. This involves chanting certain Sanskrit words with full concentration and love. They are not so much words as sound systems designed to have an effect on the environment.

There is no such thing as a mantra written in the English language because it is not a metaphysically devised language. There are only two metaphysically devised languages on Earth: one is Sanskrit and the other is secret. The basic principles of mantra are fairly easily understood. They are governed strictly according to law. With mantra you are dealing with a science which is just as strict as any physical science. The principles of mantra are based on sound vibration. It is not an expression of emotion or anything else; it is a sound vibration made by a human individual in order to bring about a certain, definite result.

Mantra is the highest known form of prayer. When mantra is spoken through or by a physical voice it has its effect upon the physical plane. The whispered mantra has its effect upon the mental plane. The mantra which is thought has its effect upon the psychic plane. In order to speak the mantra you use your voice and say it out loud. In order to whisper the mantra you again use your voice, but you should say each syllable or phrase of the mantra so quietly that anybody sitting next to you would not hear what you were saying. To think it is the hardest of all. In order to have an effect upon the psychic realms, your own aura and all types of psychic manifestations, you have to adopt a certain procedure. You have to immobilise the tongue in order to inhibit the action of the larynx. Roll the tongue backwards, putting as much pressure on it as you possibly can, until you physically feel it hurt you. Roll it up in the mouth and then press it hard against the top of the mouth. If you do not feel it hurt initially, you are not doing it correctly. When you have done this you will find that the larynx is inhibited because you cannot move the tongue. Through the immobilisation of the tongue, you then think the mantra in a pure form. Most people, even in their thoughts, are putting pressure on the larynx; they are vocalising something. You need to inhibit this sound altogether to practise silent mantra in its pure form.

Mudra for Mantra

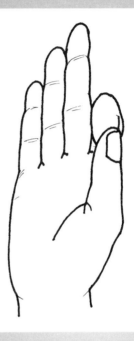

Roll the index finger of each hand back under a straight thumb and keep the other three fingers completely straight and flat upon the leg, above the knee. This hand position puts pressure on the psychic nervous system in such a way as to focus the energies within you. It is ideally used with mantra prior to prayer.

Mantra

The science of sacred sounds

The science of mantra, devised by advanced spiritual masters centuries ago, is an ancient and powerful one. Through their meditations and enhanced spiritual vision, these ancient masters were able to see and hear the action of the psychic centres within their bodies. They observed the sounds made by their activated psychic centres, or chakras, as the pranas flowed through them. From these enhanced observations they devised a sound system known as mantra. They used the ancient language of Sanskrit to record the different mantras and to pass them on to others. They knew and proved through experiment that the repetition of these sound sequences, or mantras, would enhance the natural flow of *prana* through the chakras of any individual who recited them. This enhanced flow of *prana* would then result in opening up the chakras, improving concentration, bringing inspiration and harmonising the different subtle bodies of the practitioner—all-important steps in the journey towards meditation and self-realisation.

Dr. King, as a master of this science, has agreed to give you the following five mantras, to be chanted with love and reverence. Each mantra given here has many individual characteristics which can only be discovered through practising them. You may feel more attracted to one than another, in which case you may need this one more. The first is ideal for group practice and world prayer; the second for group practice and healing; the third is a wonderful healing mantra; and the fourth, devised by Dr. King, is a joyful outpouring. They each have many other qualities as well as these. All were specifically designed to bring about a greater reaction in the higher chakras, to enhance not only your spiritual abilities but also your psychic and healing abilities. If repeated for 15 minutes or more each day, with deep love and reverence, amazing results can be achieved.

Two Dynamic Mantras

OM MANI PADME HUM

Pronounced: om manny paddmy humm

Om: as in 'from', with a short 'o' as in the first 'o' in 'Oxford'.
Mani (manny): rhymes with 'nanny'. Stress on the first syllable.
Padme (paddmy): a combination of the English words 'pad' and 'me'. Stress on the first syllable.
Hum (humm): 'u' as in 'put', not as in 'but'. Ends with a slightly longer 'm' sound.

OM RAMA HUM OM RAMA RE

Pronounced: om rah-mah humm, om rah-mah ray

Om: as above.
Rama (rah-mah): 'ra' as in 'rather'; 'ma' as in 'marker'. Both syllables carry equal stress.
Hum (humm): as above.
Re (ray): as in a 'ray of light'.

Mantras of Reverence and Soul

SOHAM SOHAM AHAM BRAHMA ASMI

Pronounced: so-ham, so-ham, ah-ham Brah-ma; ass-mee

Soham (so-ham): 'so' just like the English word 'so'; 'ham' just like the English word 'ham'. Both syllables carry equal stress.

Aham (ah-ham): 'a' as in 'father'; 'ham' as above. Both syllables carry equal stress.

Brahma (Brah-ma): 'Brah' with the 'a' as in 'father'; the 'a' of 'ma' is similar, but should be very short—almost staccato, and the pitch should be quite high.

Asmi (ass-mee): 'as' as in 'lass'; 'mi' like the English word 'me'.

OM OM OM RAMA
OM OM OM RAMA
OM OM OM RAMARA RA

Pronounced: om-om-om rah-mah; om-om-om rah-mah; om-om-om rah-mah-rah rah.

The syllables are pronounced as above. The difficult thing about this mantra is getting the right tone and rhythm. All the 'ra's and 'ma's are long, except for the penultimate 'ra' which is quite short.

In each line, the second 'om' should be slightly higher pitched than the first, and the third slightly higher pitched than the second.

A Mantra of Perfect Peace

OM SHANTI SHANTI SHANTI

Pronounced: om shanty, shanty, shanty

Om: as in the other mantras

Shanti (shanty): 'sh' as in 'she', 'anti' as in 'antimatter'. Stress on the first syllable.

This mantra is to be said once at the end of a session of spiritual practice, just before doing the Sealing Mudra, as taught on p136.

Important Notes

Always finish the mantra you are saying: never break off halfway through.

It is impossible to teach the full pronunciation of a mantra through the written word: all guidelines here have been given for speakers of standard British English. You are advised to contact the publishers for details of courses and tapes on Mantra Yoga.

The law governing mantra states that only a master of this system of yoga, such as Dr. King, can give a mantra to another person. To pass a mantra to someone before it lives within you (as it does within a master) is not in your or their interests from a mystical point of view. This principle is true of any great initiation—it is not just the passing of knowledge or information from one to another, but something much more profound than this. It is similar in principle to the apostolic succession — which can only be passed on by someone who has genuinely received it themselves in an unbroken line. Dr. King has decided to give you certain mantras to practise in the exercises section of this Initiation, should you choose to do so.

The same principle exactly is true of Mudra Yoga, the Tibetan system of adopting hand signs to channel spiritual powers. On page 145, Dr. King also gives you an ancient mudra specifically to be used in the chanting of mantra.

Giving Healing

Just as everyone can pray, so everyone can heal. Instead of raising the hands in the prayer mudra and channelling the energies outward to the world, in healing the hands are laid directly upon the patient and the energies are then channelled through the psychic centres in the palms. This is literally the laying on of hands.

Spiritual healing

On July 28th, 1956, at the Caxton Hall in London, the Master Aetherius gave the following explanation of spiritual healing in a transmission through Dr. King.

First of all, let us take a little look at what we are. Ask yourselves, 'What am I?' The answer is very simple. Indeed you are a spark of God which has, in the realm of appearance, been individualised, and that individualised particle has brought around itself certain frequencies of light which have been crystallised by applied mental pressures. That, dear friends, is the whole truth of the matter.

It is very simple, isn't it? Yes. The simplest thing in the universal system is God Itself. That is why it is the most profound thing of all. Not because of its complication, but because of its simplicity. That then, dear friends, is all you are.

You can truly say that each cell of your body is formed of different frequencies of light held together by a magnetic force which is mind. Then you must come to the startling conclusion that you are really, together with all other matter in the universe, a certain type of magnetic energy.

The journey into the atom has taught your scientists that matter is really energy held in a state of potential. We can verify this quite easily. That, dear friends, is all your body is composed of. You are so many apparently individualised magnetic units.

What then is disease? Your mystic writers have told you that disease is discomfort —disharmony—and indeed it is just that. It is that state which is caused by a certain electrical charge which has become mutated, either too strong or too weak, for a particular group of cells. This state is, of course, the direct result of Karmic Law, but from a scientific point of view, the effect itself can be described quite simply.

I should like to say of your medical scientists that they will never find the real answer to discomfort—disease—until they reorientate their methods of investigation. Do you not see that your science—your medical science—is far too complicated?

When your medical back-room boys recognise the fact that cellular structure is only a certain form of light held in a definite state by a primeval force, a magnetic force which you call mind, they will then have to start a new system of treatment based upon the application of the correct light frequencies—in other words, colour. Is it not simple? Of course it is.

Now then, what has all this to do with so-called spiritual healing? It has everything to do with it. All forms of spiritual and religious healing, faith healing or prayer healing by touch, are really healings brought about by the addition or subtraction of certain magnetic charges to certain cellular groups.

The cells in a human body are fed, as you know, through the lymphatic passages and the bloodstream, and by the absorption of gases through the lungs into the lymph and blood circulatory systems. Within all food you eat there is a magnetic potential. The difference between an ordinary piece of food and something which is called a vitamin is a certain magnetic charge. Vitamins are those little scraps of acid, alkali or salts which contain a very powerful magnetic potential and this magnetic potential is

released to the cellular structure through the digestive process. The difference between ordinary food and food containing certain valuable chemical and mineral properties, is basically one of magnetic potential.

That is why certain foods do you very much good; these foods are classed as being full of vitamin so-and-so. It is really that they contain certain magnetic power which can be absorbed and used by the mind potential of the whole, operating through groups of cellular structure.

Now, a human body, when governed by the deeper feelings—the higher type of magnetism—becomes virtually a transmitting station and it can transmit various types of magnetic energy from itself to another human body which needs this charge.

So what, then, is spiritual healing?

This is what it is: it is the transmission of required—note, required—magnetic energy from and through—note that, from and through—the body of the healer to the patient. Certain healers have a quality which allows them to see, quite clearly, what type of energy is necessary, and this energy is requested or demanded, either consciously or superconsciously, by the healer from the universal supply; and this energy then flows through the nervous system and cellular structure of the healer and out to the patient.

Now some healers work quite consciously. They know that a particular vibration is needed and they attract to themselves this magnetic vibration and transmit it to a group of cellular structures in the physical body of the patient often via his etheric and astral bodies. Others, such as faith healers and people who work with prayer, do not realise this, but they know that to pray to God gives them a certain power. When they pray to God, of course, they make a demand on certain energies—and those energies, if they pray with the right motive, are given to them so that they virtually become transmitting stations for those energies which are radiated outward and are received into the body of the patient.

Isn't it simple? Isn't it easy? Now can you understand it? There is nothing complicated about it, nothing weird or wondrous about it—not at all.

Some religious factors would tell you that they and they only are allowed to give healing. This, of course, is childish nonsense. There is not a man, woman or a young person in the hall this evening who cannot give some form of healing. If their healing is not effective then it is because they are not pure enough as a channel, or that they are very much run down, or that they do not know, either consciously or superconsciously, how to make the correct demands upon their own potential and the potential existing within the universal supply.

Now let me answer the great mystery question. Right down through the ages it has come—'Physician, why can't you heal yourself?' Well, of course, the physician, the healer, can heal himself very often, but not always. He may be considered good at giving other people healing and yet not seem to be able to move the same complaint from himself. This is, in the main, due to the fact that he would not dream of expending as much energy on giving himself healing as he would in transmitting it to an ailing patient. That is one factor.

There is another one though. You see, the cellular structure is so made that it reacts to a force which may be called a 'reaction force.' Now let us suppose a healer needs a certain magnetic potential in his shoulder. If he rubs it himself that will do some good, but if somebody else rubs the part for him, it will do more good. Why? Because the cellular structure in the shoulder is being charged through a certain turbulence caused by the bringing together of two—we can call them—separate magnetic poles. In other words, there is a certain reaction there.

Any sensitive person knows that if another person touches him he has a different feeling than if he touches himself, and yet that other touch may have produced almost the same magnetic stimulation as his own touch—but it feels different. That is because of this almost primeval reactory principle, inherent in cellular structure, as well as within the mind or soul which governs the function of that structure. A healer touches himself—he is used to touching himself—a familiar magnetic action is brought about. However, someone else touches him in the same spot and his mind registers the feeling in a different way and thus causes a reaction to take place within the cellular structure, and that reaction in turn causes a more definite

absorption of the needed energy. Isn't it simple? Oh yes, it certainly is. There is nothing complicated about it.

If you think about some of the things I have said—really work them out in your own mind—then you will have a different outlook. You will see that no matter how apparently complicated your disease is, the correct magnetic power can put it right. Virtually, what I am saying is this—that there is no such thing as an incurable disease.

Dr. George King has developed a powerful spiritual healing technique, easily learned by all, either through his excellent textbook, *You Too Can Heal*, or through courses held by The Aetherius Society throughout the world. Already thousands have learned how to give effective spiritual healing with this easy to learn technique, often with miraculous results. Giving spiritual healing to others can also bring about an essential balancing of spiritual energy within the healer, which can be very important once one begins to practise some of the advanced spiritual practices described within this book.

Spiritual healing can also be given if you are not able to give healing through the laying on of hands. It can be done over a distance (absent healing) in the following way:

In practising absent healing, try to visualise the patient as being perfect. Try not to see the person as having anything wrong with them. If you do, then immediately counteract that by charging them with a brilliant white light.

Charge them with an energy but do not see any complaint. Try to visualise them as being perfect. Perhaps they have something wrong with the spine and they cannot move one of their limbs. You have seen that and you cannot erase it from the memory. The memory cells from the subconscious hold that picture and the conscious mind, too, holds that picture.

Start to concentrate on them as being healed and completely well. Do not try to tell yourself a lie. You cannot say, "I have not seen the spine diseased," because you have. The memory will come before you and immediately you concentrate on them, you are going to see them as you last saw them physically—as having something wrong with them. But immediately, imagine them charged with a great white flame and see the spine relaxed. See them get up and walk about and run around. Imagine them filled with joy and happiness. The more you do this, the greater will be your healing, for you are doing two things: you are visualising that they are healed, and you are impressing on their thoughts that they are healed.

First of all you should say an inspirational prayer; something you feel you should say. Pray to whatever Divine Source you have faith in. If it was me, I would pray to Brahma; on the other hand, you might wish to pray to God, or even a Master like Jesus. You may even want to pray to your higher self or the higher self of the person who is sick. Choose the source of the energy and then put out your hands with arms outstretched and really pray. Give it all you have got, then about 50% more, until you feel the flow of energy through your body. If you have a degree of clairvoyance you will see the energy flowing through you and out through the palms of the hands and heart centre.

While you are praying, try to visualise your patient. Try to imagine an image of them as being perfect. Do not allow yourself to see one blemish on them. When you have this visualisation, try to hold it while saying the prayer and visualise them being charged with the energy coming through you. Visualise the energy as being white; never try to modify the colour of the energy—always make it white. Then, thank the source for this energy, and also for giving you the divine privilege of being able to act as a channel.

Then detach. It is done, it is finished; the patient is better. If you hear the next day that they are not better, or only a little better, go through the same procedure again. Then detach until the next time you choose to go through the same procedure. As you continue you will be able to work yourself up into such a state that eventually you will not have to perform the procedure more than once or twice. So-called miracles are brought about in this way.

It is at this stage that you perform the Sealing Mudra, as described on page 136.

Colour Healing

In spiritual healing, it is always best to visualise the power as a white light, since white includes all the colours of the spectrum. For specific ailments, selected colours radiated by a colour lamp or projector can also be very beneficial. This is the science of chromotherapy or colour healing.

Colour healing is simple, yet effectively enhances all manipulative and spiritual healing treatments. There are several potent colours, of which the most important are green, yellow, orange, red, blue and violet. I will now explain a little about the use of each colour vibration so that readers may use this information for the promotion of better well-being and harmony within themselves. Always apply colour vibrations on the bare skin after you have received any other treatments necessary.

An Introduction to Healing with Colour

Green – the harmoniser

This is the most basic colour of all in healing. It is the colour which you always use first and last. No matter what you are ailing from, start off and finish with an application of green for 10 minutes each. It is the safest colour of all to use. It is a colour which can be applied all over yourself or it can be concentrated onto any one part of the body. The green should be taken from the middle of the colour spectrum, neither too blue nor too yellow. You should have the type of colour lamp that will spread out the light so that it can be played all over the front and back. Green is the colour of balance, which harmonises the flow of *prana*, or universal life force, throughout the psychic centres. As green is the great balancer and harmoniser it causes many people to become very relaxed. It tends to counteract subtle energies which have built up in one nerve ganglia and caused the starvation of another nerve ganglia. It operates, as do all other colours, firstly on the aura. The reflection of it then reacts upon the physical body. You must be relaxed while the green light bathes the whole front of the body for five minutes and the back for five minutes. Then you can start using other colours.

Yellow – for the mind

Yellow is the colour which signifies wisdom. Any mental deficiency, no matter how it shows itself, will be relieved by the use of yellow if concentrated onto small areas of the body. A concentrated beam of yellow light, about the size of a tennis ball, applied at the base and at the front of the neck, has been found very valuable for all cases of nervous conditions and for all cases where some mental blockage or other shows itself. The mental blockage may be brought on by bad circulation which caused the brain cells to be starved of lymph and blood. It may be caused by incorrect breathing, which brings about mental deterioration more quickly than anything else; or it may be the result of a nervous breakdown or severe mental strain. In the latter case, it could no longer be considered a mental blockage. Yellow is the colour which will relieve this type of condition. The normal time of application is 12 minutes altogether. If it is applied over the front and back of the head and the front and back of the neck in concentrated form, it should last for three minutes on each place on the bare skin. Ladies should remove their make-up before colour healing as the pigments are liable to reflect the colour rays which are extremely subtle in nature.

The Healing Power of Orange

The stimulator

This is a stimulating colour which can be given to the spleen, liver, kidneys, heart, and to any organ which helps to promote good circulation. The total time for application is 10 minutes. Apply a bright orange vibration in concentrated form to the spleen if you are suffering with low circulatory trouble, but not if you suffer with high blood pressure. All the internal organs, such as liver, kidneys, bowels, can be stimulated by this colour. The more concentrated it is, the more effective it will be. Your colour apparatus should be good enough to concentrate a beam of light down to about the size of a tennis ball. Such a concentrated beam of orange vibration played for four minutes on the spleen twice per week will help those with low circulatory trouble. This colour will help to stimulate the heart if concentrated over this place, or any other organ which needs stimulation. Orange is the great vitaliser, and if given in conjunction with spiritual healing and other forms of natural treatments, it can often supplement them and act as a trigger. Do not apply orange to the forehead of anyone who is highly nervous. If you or your patient suffers from brain fatigue, orange can be given on the back of the neck, but not for longer than four minutes.

Red – the Lowest Vibration

The energiser

Bright crimson red is even a more potent stimulator than orange. This should not be given to anyone on the head. If concentrated on rheumatic joints, it will be beneficial. You can apply the red to the legs, knees or ankles for 10 or 15 minutes. If the rheumatic conditions are high up in the shoulders, I would suggest an application for only five minutes at a time. Place your lamp in such a way that the beam will be projected onto the back or front of the shoulder and not come across the shoulder onto the head. If it does shine on the head it is not harmful in any way, but it is best to avoid this. As the light frequencies of red are slow and very long, they have high penetrating properties, therefore can be used to stimulate the aura (and physical body) to such an extent that circulatory blockages can be cleared. The colour red can be given over the liver, kidneys or bladder for three minutes without any harm whatever. Keep the colour red away from the head of a patient who has had a nervous breakdown or who is highly strung in any way. Infrared, too, can be used very successfully. An infrared lamp is based on the same principle as an ordinary red colour lamp, except that the very potent infrared rays act directly upon the physical body by causing great heat. Infrared is far more dangerous to use than the colour red and should not be given for longer than 15 minutes on any part of the body. Infrared rays should not be given over the reproductive organs of a man or a woman, neither should they be given for more than two minutes over the liver, kidneys or bladder, because they can cause some damage. Do not under any account give infrared rays to the head, certainly not the eyes. If you are using infrared, then strictly obey your doctor's recommendations.

The Calming Vibrations

Blue – the relaxant

The most effective shade is a deep, full-bodied primary blue and this can be applied from the top of the head to the feet of most sufferers. If the complaint is high blood pressure, any kind of nervous breakdown, nervous tension in any one of its forms, blue applied for 10 minutes can be beneficial. On the other hand, if you suffer from a cold or flu, use orange in preference to blue because you will discover, especially if you are sensitive, that you are liable to get physically cold under the application of a blue light. This is caused because the high vibrations are short and quick and they manifest as cold rather than heat. Orange and red produce heat and are necessary in cases of low temperature; blue produces coldness and is necessary in cases of high temperature. Blue causes most people to relax. An application of blue colour vibrations will also help people to sleep who suffer with mild insomnia. For more severe cases, a low wattage dark blue light in the bedroom can prove beneficial.

Violet – the cleanser

Violet can be used all over the body. I suggest that violet light is confined to the upper parts of the body and mainly to the forehead, the back and front of the head, the back and front of the neck, and in concentrated form over the heart and between the shoulder blades, for a total time of 15 minutes. Violet tends to bring relaxation and, like blue, can often be felt as waves of coldness. It does not stimulate basic circulation, but it does stimulate the flow of the more subtle energies throughout the psychic centres and the nervous system. Because of this it is especially beneficial when used on the forehead and neck.

Colour Through the Eyes

Stimulating the brain through direct application of light

Another aspect of colour healing, which should be done very carefully, is the introduction of colour through the eyes. We all know that what we see affects us. What most people do not realise is that every colour seen has some effect upon the cells of the body.

Green can safely be introduced through the eyes. When you start your colour treatment with green, look at the green light for a couple of minutes. When you use violet, blue or yellow, do the same with these colours and you will find that they will have a great inspirational effect upon you. I do not suggest that you look at orange or red light because of its basic vibrational properties. If your colour lamp is too bright to look at without any eye strain whatever, then some kind of a diffusing screen should be put in front of it while you look at it. If this is not possible, then project the colour on a movie screen if you have one, or even a white sheet, while you look at it for two minutes.

When we projected a violet light onto a screen in front of people who were performing the violet flame practice, every one of them remarked how much easier it was to do this practice when they could actually see this colour. At least a dozen people remarked how relaxed and harmonious they felt afterwards. You could use this before the practice of The Twelve Blessings. At the end of your practice throw a green light on the same screen for a couple of minutes and this will enhance the procedure.

More About Colour

What materials to use and the deeper aspects of the therapy

The success of colour healing does, to some extent, depend on the purity of the colour and the power of the lamp behind it. Plastic colour material can be obtained from any theatrical equipment depot, which can easily be cut to any size you require. We have found a good type to be fireproof cinemoid. It is heat resistant and very tough. There are excellent colour healing lamps for sale, some of which are expensive because they are hand-built of the finest materials available. But it is not necessary to pay a lot of money for a piece of apparatus. Any slide projector can be used as an excellent colour vibration lamp. It can be focused and does not give out undue heat. Coloured plastic can be mounted in the slide carriers between glass and most of these projectors have an effective cooling system. You can use remote control to enable you to set up your colours first and then push the button when you want to change the colour. You should use a lamp between 250 and 500 watts, but never over 500 watts. If your apparatus is a powerful slide projector you will not be able to look at it and take the colour through the eyes, but you can project the colour most effectively onto a screen.

There is a deep occult significance behind all colours. Some astrologers have worked out the colour combinations which correspond to birth signs. This information from a reliable source can be incorporated into your treatment. Colour healing can supplement all other forms of spiritual healing, as well as orthodox methods of healing.

Sometimes colour healing acts quickly, but not always. As a general rule, the more spiritually attuned the user is, the more effect colour vibrations will have, but even a relatively insensitive person will eventually react to this treatment. So persist with it even though it appears, as it will in some cases, to be slow in its reaction. In some countries there have been strict laws prohibiting the use of colour healing professionally, except by qualified medical practitioners. This information is not designed to be used professionally, but to give you sufficient knowledge about colour vibrations to give yourself a treatment should you wish to do so.

The Protective Practice

Here is a beautiful practice for radiating spiritual powers whenever you need protection from anger, jealousy or other unpleasant vibrations directed towards you.

The Master Aetherius

If someone greatly upsets you, do not continue a useless, hot-tempered argument with them. Stand perfectly still, hands at sides and slightly clenched; balance the body on the balls of your feet by bending your knees very slightly. Look your opponent straight in the eyes and whisper to yourself mentally, with all the feeling you can muster, 'God bless the eyesight of so-and-so.' Fill in their full name if you know it. If you do this correctly then no one can do you any harm. This is a simple practice but often needs great self-control for correct performance. I feel sure that regular performance of this spiritual exercise will teach you all an extremely valuable lesson in tolerance. There is nothing negative at all about it, for by doing these things you must send a calming current of spiritual power towards the other, which will act like healing balm on a sore spot. All his hate will be consumed in the fires of your love.

The eyes are the mirrors of the soul. By sending a blessing of love towards the eyes of one who bears you malice, you are virtually blessing the very soul of that person. You are returning good for evil. In fact, you are proving your faith in the Divine Creator by the recognition that even an antagonist is a brother to be blessed and healed. Like all the other mystical practices, this one also works, sometimes in almost a magical way. How many times have you been hurt by the burning scorn in the eyes of another? Action and reaction are opposite and equal. Therefore, if the very eyes which are clouded by hate or scorn see tolerance reflected by yours, this reaction cancels out the action of the other. The result is predetermined by your reaction, which is opposite to that of the other. Even an animal knows this. How many of you have started to scold your dog until that dog looks you straight in the eyes? Is not your heart filled with forgiveness? You all know the answer to that.

By radiating spiritual powers to others, you will light a flame in your heart which will inspire you towards the greatest of all callings: that of giving global service.

Of all the yogas I have studied, Karma Yoga is the greatest yoga of all.

It is Karma Yoga which will save the world.

Dr. George King

The Sixth Initiation
Giving Global Service

Karma Yoga

This Initiation is the shortest and yet, in many ways, the most important in the book. Service is the key to the new millennium. With it, we can build a fantastic new age of peace and enlightenment; without it, we certainly will not at this time in our history. For the individual it is the best possible way to manipulate your personal karmic pattern in the most beneficial manner.

Despite the many tomes of Sanskrit lore devoted to the subject of karma, never has the main essential principle of spiritual evolution been so simply expressed as in the phrase: "Manipulate your karmic pattern." Immediately a new emphasis is introduced. The individual can control his or her own karma. Karma, after all, is a scientific, natural force—a Law which the individual can

personally cooperate with for the spiritual benefit of himself and others. It can be manipulated through service to others.

Service is a duty. It is human decency to help others. It is also, according to Karmic Law, beneficial to the server. A spiral of evolution and growth is created through unselfish

Never has the main essential principle of spiritual evolution been so simply expressed as in the phrase: "Manipulate your karmic pattern."

service. Through serving others, step-by-step the individual progresses, advances, becomes more enlightened and gains greater freedom from limitation. There is one overriding necessity: a pure, unselfish motive. For it is through motivation that the process works. It is not some form of divine intervention but a natural, scientific procedure. The individual must advance, must become more spiritually evolved, more healthy, with more freedom from basic worry than he would have had, if he serves with the right motive. These evolutionary factors exist within a framework of more than one life, though at times the results are felt immediately.

The greatest service is given to the world as a whole, not just to the individual, since far more good can be done for far more people in this way. The greatest yoga and the greatest religious act is the dispensation of spiritual energy to the world as a whole. Cooperation with missions and spiritual practices designed to send out spiritual energy to the world is the most effective form of service in these days. Since it is the most powerful form of service, it must also be a guaranteed path of spiritual advancement, as a result of the karma which is manipulated by the individual who serves in this way.

Service is an absolutely safe way of raising *kundalini*, though probably slower than other ways. It will, however, help mankind and give you a wonderful balance. It will undoubtedly bring about a release of *kundalini*. It may be only a partial release of the energy at a time, but it will bring about a great balance in your life—and the after-life will be enhanced, when the rewards are given out whether we expect them or not. Any service that you perform, especially in these days, goes very definitely in your favour. Service to others is one sure and balanced way of raising and activating this great primordial force, which gradually opens each psychic centre. You have to temper your journey within with true regard for the suffering of your fellow men. Service is essential. If anyone in the world decides to cut himself off from civilisation and go into a retreat so that he can gain ecstatic bliss, and hopes that he will get out of reincarnation and prepare for his ascension, he will fail.

Times have changed—the emphasis in all spiritual practice nowadays must include a concern for others as well as yourself. The highest stage of meditation reveals a oneness with the whole. It would be patently absurd to try to ignore the whole in order to reach this stage of oneness with it. There was a time when an allowance was made within the Karmic Law for an individual to do so, but now, with all the potential dangers to human existence through nuclear experimentation, pollution and other technological so-called advances, no such allowance can be made. Service and self-development are as essential to each other as breathing out and breathing in. You simply cannot do one without the other.

This means that the greatest form of yoga to practise in the new millennium is Karma Yoga—the yoga of service.

Thousands of years ago it used to be the yoga solely to try to attain meditation [*samadhi*]. There has been a great change in the world over the last few centuries. At the time of Buddha, the advice given to the aspirant was to search for concentration, contemplation and meditation, so that he could enhance his own personal development and then be of service to his fellow men. The masters have not so much changed their advice now, as quickened it up. If everyone made up their minds to search only for personal development before they could be of service, it could take 20 or 30 lives. So, we have to speed things up. To some extent we may sacrifice our own personal development on the rock of Karma Yoga, or Union with God through Service.

Raja Yoga gives you certain practices which enhance your psychic capabilities. When you really can use them, you detach from them and bring that power into a higher centre. Most psychics see through the solar plexus. If you bring the power into a higher centre, you go into a state of bliss. Basic states of *samadhi* are states of imperturbable bliss. If you go on pushing your abilities by doing certain practices, you can go into the deep samadhic states of meditation. In these states you receive great enlightenment, as well as this bliss. When you are good enough, you can stay in it for an hour, two hours, a day, 50 years or 150 years. Your body does not age in this state. Gnani Yoga is probably an even higher form of yoga than Raja. It includes Raja Yoga up to the point of meditation. The meditator takes a *samadhi*, or deep meditative state, on many different aspects of truth and becomes a wise person. He has great knowledge and power.

Karma Yoga is very different from these. It is done by people who, on the face of it, are fool enough to take on the worries and woes of others. Such a person does the

Virtual novices are achieving the selfsame results that the adepts of a few hundred years ago did.

exact opposite from the Raja Yogi who cuts himself off from mankind and all his worries and woes, in order to gain bliss. A Karma Yogi goes in among mankind, serving them in many different ways. The result of this is sometimes the opposite of the deep states of bliss. In these days, such is the state of the Earth that service is the pathway for mankind. What time you may seem to lose of the blissful states now, you will gain in the blissful states later by Karmic Law. If anything, this is the most difficult path, because it can only be trod by real people, who have burned out of themselves the cancer of selfishness. You cannot perform Karma Yoga and be selfish at the same time. This cancer must first be healed within yourself. One of the great exponents of Karma Yoga was Jesus. He demonstrated it right through his life in thousands of different ways.

The more advanced you become, the more you can serve, but we cannot wait until we are advanced before we begin to serve. You should perform what Raja Yoga you can, and all the Karma Yoga you can in these days. Every initiate on Earth is being given a job in these days equal to what the old masters were given, even though he is only an initiate. Every possible channel for healing and teaching that can be used is being used to its fullest extent. Relatively unenlightened people are coming forward and giving inspirational messages, wonderful healing and so on. Virtual novices are achieving the selfsame results that the adepts of a few hundred years ago did with healing, and that is only one branch of metaphysical science. There are people being used for inspirational messages who know nothing at all about the science behind it. They are virtual jewels of people who, because they are fairly clean, pure channels, are being used to bring forth many wonderful Karma Yoga results in these days.

In these days, Karma Yoga, or service to others, is the main yoga. All else is second place. Even the great Raja is second place. Gnani is second place. At one time, to me, Raja was everything; Gnani was everything. I did not ever consider Karma as being of very much use, save for people who were not mentally equipped to study Raja and Gnani. It was not easy for an ignorant person like myself to make this change within themselves. It may not be easy for some of you to make it, but it is possible. It can be done and once it is done, then you are on the path. And the divine promise is this: for every hour you give up a meditative state, in future lives you will spend maybe a hundred hours in the same state.

If you would do yourself and others a good turn and help the masters to bring their Cosmic Plan into being in the new millennium, you would equip yourself to the best of your ability now. You would do healing, prayer, spiritual teaching, help the old, the blind and infirm, and take part in any one or all of the hundreds of forms of different service which are so desperately needed on Earth in these days.

The divine promise is this: for every hour you give up a meditative state, in future lives you will spend maybe a hundred hours in the same state.

Service in the New Age

One of the things which marks out the spiritually advanced person in these days is their sense of responsibility. Not just a sense of responsibility for their own domestic and professional affairs, which is really a basic minimum, but for those they have never met; for conditions on the other side of the globe; for all life on the planet. Such a person is willing to make sacrifices and work with others to bring the greatest possible benefit to the whole. The following transmission, channelled through Dr. King by a cosmic intelligence from Mars in 1961, summarises this greatest of all callings. It is the third in the series known as The Nine Freedoms.

The greatest yoga is Service.

The greatest religion is Service.

The greatest act
is that act
done in Service.

The Third Freedom

The Third Freedom

Freedom from selfishness is Service.

In these days there is much Service which is vitally important to Terra. There are few servers.

Service is a culmination of experiences which denote the server as being on the ladder of evolution, firmly on this ladder.

Those who have a yearning desire to serve and indeed are doing so, are those who have slain selfishness; are those who are gradually overcoming their lower materialistic aspects; are those who are sometimes slowly, but nevertheless surely, advancing towards enlightenment.

In these days upon Terra, it is selfless action, called Service which will count in your initiations of tomorrow. Your Service to others will be known and you will judge yourselves accordingly.

If you would burn up your lower Karmic aspects, you would serve.

If you would, at this very moment, begin to build tomorrow's temple upon the sure foundations of today's right action, you would serve.

If you would be free from the materialistic prison cunningly devised to enslave you, you would serve.

If you would be detached from your own petty worries, you would serve.

If you would enjoy better health, you would serve.

If you would prepare yourselves for the new world, you would serve.

Service is indeed a glorious undertaking! It is lasting, for every act of Service is written in everlasting letters of fire in the Akashic Book. When you walk into the halls of self-judgement, you will read what your own hand hath written upon these pages and by the immutable Law of Karma, you will accordingly set limitation upon your rebirth.

Break away from your own troubles by concentrating upon the sufferings of others.

Serve in the great spiritual battle and you can walk with head high and stand in any hall unafraid to read what be written there.

The greatest yoga is Service.

The greatest religion is Service.

The greatest act is that act done in Service.

Kill possession. Transmute selfishness into Service for others and your reward will come. Enlightenment, like the break of dawn upon the darkest night, will cast the shadows of this night before it.

Serve—and you will become enlightened.

Serve—and you will be practising true selfless love.

Serve—and the mighty power of *kundalini* will rise in natural, unforced fashion and open the chakra jewels in your higher bodies. In will pour inspiration and you will be standing on the verge of the initiation into adeptship.

There are no words great enough to describe the wonder of Service.

And no words can describe the crime of selfishness.

Know this. Whether you like it or not does not matter, it is the truth. I, Mars, do declare it as such. If you believe it not today, terrestrial man, you will know it in your morrow.

What is Service but love in practical action.

Service is the result of applied spiritual logic. It is the lasting flower in the garden of enlightenment.

Service is the jewel in the rock of attainment.

There are many ways to serve upon Terra. Look around you and see: ignorance, suffering, want, hate, greed, selfishness, war, murder, robbery, violence in every form. See how people, the young ones, are being deluded.

There are many ways indeed to serve.

By your Service, you can help to heal those who are sick, and you should.

By your Service, you can help to give encouragement and strength to those who are depressed and weak, and you should do this.

By your Service, you can throw a dazzling beam of scintillating, white, vibrant energy into the darkness of a suffering world and raise it.

It is—by God, it is—the jewel in the rock of attainment.

It is the great practice in these days.

One person who is rendering true, spiritual Service—not self delusion, but true, spiritual Service—to those who need it, is worth ten who retreat from the suffering of others in order to bring about a state of joy and peace within themselves.

This declaration do I throw into every mental realm. I would inform those aspirants who, in total disregard of human needs, retreat into the wilderness: 'Come you hence, for you are fools!'

Service, my friends, is greatness.

Serve and be great! Nay—be everlasting.

Dr. King once summed up the greatness of service in the following way:

A lot of people call me a master of yoga. They ask me what kind of yogas I have studied and I tell them. There is one yoga which I should talk more about and that is Karma Yoga. Of all the yogas I have studied, Karma Yoga is the greatest of all. It is Karma Yoga which will save the world. The other yogas are necessary to obtain the powers and to get the inspiration, but then you must use your powers and inspiration for the benefit of all. They must be brought into living manifestation in order to be of any good to the world.

Only when the lesson of global service is truly learned will you be able to attain the thing we are all here to realise, namely—enlightenment.

**Serve—and the mighty power of kundalini
will rise in natural, unforced fashion
and open the chakra jewels
in you higher bodies.**

**In will pour inspiration
and you will be standing on the verge
of the initiation into adeptship.**

The Nine Freedoms

The Seventh Initiation
Attaining Enlightenment

Yoga Philosophy

According to ancient writings, the goal of all yoga practice is to attain enlightenment. The great aphorisms of Sri Patanjali, the advanced Buddhist teachings and, before either of these, the Vedic writings, emphasise this single-minded quest for personal perfection. Along the way, psychic and mystical powers would be gained, which are referred to by Patanjali as *siddhis*. There are yogis alive today who can materialise objects, thus proving the power of mind over matter; others can demonstrate psychic vision (remote viewing) over thousands of miles accurately; others can demonstrate telepathy or psychokinesis under laboratory conditions. But these types of ability, according to yoga philosophy, should only be steps along the road to enlightenment.

Too many fall into the trap of getting stuck at this stage and become nothing more than highly sophisticated conjurers. The true yogi rejects these mental and physical displays of inner power to go even further within and realise their true potential, namely, enlightenment.

In this new millennium, it is essential to give service to others. This is the very essence of spiritual expression and therefore crucial to all forms of development. In former times a karmic allowance was made to attract aspirants to the path, and to ensure that a certain number, tiny though it was in comparison to the mass of humanity, became advanced enough to help the masters to hold the light on Earth. But there was often a missing element in traditional yoga philosophy—namely, the overriding importance of service. It was known that as

Advanced Exercises

A few words about the practices contained in this section

This Seventh Initiation is for those advanced students who wish to go all the way on the path of spiritual development.

The exercises it contains should only be practised in the context of a life of balanced spirituality and service.

If you practise them, you will gradually start to raise the *kundalini*, and so you must be sure to follow every step of each practice as taught.

Providing you do so, regular performance of these wonderful, powerful, advanced practices will place you firmly on the path to enlightenment.

the aspirant advanced, he would become so inspired with love and compassion that he would want to help others at least as much as himself. The higher states of consciousness lead to a deep awareness that we are all one and, since we are all one, there is no sense in concentrating exclusively on your own development. But in these days, a new urgency has been introduced. To quote Dr. King:

Go towards God now! Even a saint cannot reclaim a wasted minute.

Service should become the cornerstone of yoga philosophy.

By the same token, though, some who serve neglect their own development too much. They think that it will take care of itself as though it requires no effort. Such people tend to burn out on the spiritual path and, in the end, serve far less than they would have done if they had included more self-development instead of just serving others. It is like breathing: the in-breath (inspiration) is self-development and the out-breath (expiration) is service. You cannot do one without the other—they are completely interdependent. It is true that some are called to serve and have very little opportunity at times to concentrate on themselves.

But such times are not indefinite—the opportunity to develop will always come to you and then you should take it.

At one time—and some still teach this now—it was advocated that a yoga student should choose the path to which he was most suited. It might be Raja, Gnani, Karma or Bhakti, depending on his particular characteristics and aptitudes. There is wisdom in this, but also a flaw which in this new millennium needs to be rectified. It is now not so much a question of which path suits you, but more which path will enable you to do the most good for the world as a whole. Choosing the right path will set the best karmic framework for your development to take place.

Meditation

Dr. King has the highest standards I have encountered in his definition of true samadhic meditation.

Meditation is that state in which he who contemplates becomes one with that upon which he contemplates. It is a state which is contacted almost always in a very deep trance state. There are only rare cases of meditation where meditation itself is gained while the subject is conscious. It is a state where the consciousness of the individual, the superconsciousness of the individual, contacts the all-knowledge space within that individual. The soul of the individual is bathed in the light radiated by the spirit, or spark of God, within. You will never touch that source, but you can come near to it and bathe the soul in the light of this spirit. When you come out of a state of meditation, you come out as a knower, a person who knows about that upon which you meditated.

Of all the words in the English language that are used wrongly, meditation is used more wrongly than almost any other word. I have heard people say that their idea of meditation was sitting knitting, looking into the fire in a kind of abstracted way. That is not meditation at all. It is not even true contemplation. When a person has experienced meditation, he knows it beyond all shadow of doubt. It is the most highly elevated state of consciousness which a person can gain.

Contemplation is quite a long step for man to take, but meditation is a very much longer one. When you practise concentration, you begin to make the great

power of *kundalini* rise, gently and slowly—which is the safest way to do it—up the spine and into a higher psychic centre. In contemplation you make the *kundalini* rise to a higher psychic centre still—to the solar plexus centre, and even partially up to the heart centre. But in meditation you have to bring *kundalini* up to at least the throat centre. When *kundalini* begins to manifest in the heart centre you begin to get into the deeper steps of meditation. When it begins to manifest in the throat centre, and particularly, the christ centre, you will then enter into the deepest state of meditation. You might stay in meditation for a long time or fractions of a second.

From a purely physical point of view, in a meditative state the person who is meditating enters into a deep trance state, unable to walk, because *kundalini* has left the lower centres and so has the energy left the lower centres and is manifesting above the heart centre, and you enter a state of immobility of body. Gradually you enter a state of immobility of mind, too. First the state of immobility of body is most noticeable. You cannot walk; the heart stops functioning, or the beats may be just imperceptible, but rigor mortis will not set in. Even if you raise *kundalini* in its entirety, entering the deepest state of trance possible to all mankind, still rigor mortis will not set in because you leave a band of heat around the top of the head, which will keep the blood warm enough to stop rigor mortis. You enter a death-like state without dying. Meditation is a state of conscious death where you, the person meditating, are released from the limitations of the physical body. In this state you may project your consciousness onto high planes. You may pick up a particular object, like a holy book. You already know through your concentration all the information in it. Through your contemplation you already know even the atomic structure from which the book is made. But meditation will take you very much further than even this, to virtually abstract realms. You will know why the author saw fit to write that book when he did; what spiritual significance it has to mankind; why it was written at the time it was, and so on. You would come back out of meditation and say, "I know about that." You would return as a knower, rather than a person who said, "This is my opinion." You can then honestly, before man and God say, in a humble, gentle manner, "I know this to be so." You would not argue about it; you may not even be prepared to discuss it, but you would indeed know it to be so.

It is only after samadhic meditation has been experienced, that a person can be described as fully enlightened.

Enlightenment is more than knowledge or even intelligence, though both these follow from it. The following technical description of meditation by Dr. King is based on his personal experience of the state.

Meditation is only brought about when the all-important power of *kundalini* is risen consciously up the spinal column of the aspirant. It rises from the base chakra, penetrates the sex centre, and moves higher to the solar plexus. As it is moved upwards, it takes all the power from the sex centre, which becomes dormant. It is then moved, consciously, up into the heart centre. As it pierces the heart centre, the solar plexus centre is devoid of its energy and this becomes dormant. At this stage the meditator becomes paralysed, unable to walk. When the power is taken from the nerve ganglia which act as a pranic battery in the solar plexus and is risen up to the heart centre, he is no longer able to move his legs and hips. When the power pierces the heart centre, the chakra then blossoms forth and the tremendous power of love can for the first time be understood and radiated to all in need. At this stage, the aspirant is capable of advanced psychic vision. He is able to hear the forces within this vortex of power. Some of these forces sound to him like a giant bell which is tolling, and often he will

A Meditation

If you are capable of meditation, you will learn much from this statement:

God is the only eternal simple in the universe.

If there was anything else in the universe besides God it would mean complexity, and by logic and law, that could not be endured.

Take that into your meditations with you and I think you will come out a thousand years older than you are now.

hear this so loudly, that it will appear to do his ear drums actual physical damage. There is a tremendous strain put upon the centre and if the heart is weak, it can be damaged by severe palpitation; or if the student who is raising the *kundalini* has not completely controlled the baser aspects of life, he will bring these energies up into the heart centre and cause his heart to be diseased for life. As well as this, if the lower part of his body has some ailment, he will actually transfer the vibrations of this condition to the heart centre and give himself an incurable heart disease. If, however, the aspirant has overcome these things and he is then able to raise, consciously, the great power of *kundalini* into the throat centre, the heart centre is, by the magnetic attraction of the *kundalini*, devoid of energy and the physical heart nearly stops beating. Now the aspirant is sitting absolutely and completely immobile.

He or she is in a very deep state of trance. The base, sex, solar plexus and heart centres have had all the power taken from them and they are not operating. The aspirant is unable to move physically, because he is completely paralysed. The blood has almost stopped circulation around the body, because the heart beats have almost ceased, or in some cases, actually physically stopped. The aspirant is, to all intents and purposes, in a state of conscious death. But the intuition has not stopped. Inner, shining light and deep vision are being experienced now. Highly elevated mental energies are now being drawn into the throat centre and the meditator is beginning to understand and appreciate the irrevocable occult laws for the first time. Inside, there is all vibrant activity. He can hear the tremendous vortex of power within the christ centre above, which physically sounds to him like the rushing waters of a gigantic waterfall. In fact, at first he cannot hear anything else except this. Then, as he becomes more attuned, he hears the subtle symphony of life. He can hear a tree growing, a man talk to another miles away. He can hear a cloud form 2,000 feet above him if he thinks about it. His hearing becomes so acute that he can hear the subtle sounds of whatever he dwells upon. He can even hear the screeching, high-pitched whine caused by a beam of light as it careers through the envelope of gas molecules which surround the planet. If he meditates upon this supersonic sound, he can become aware of the resonating harmonics caused as the photons of light are reflected from any object, sounding like a delicately blended symphonic pattern of musical notes which seem, in some strange way, to radiate from all sources at once, yet echo and re-echo as though passing on through some gigantic tunnel.

He can transfer his hearing above the atmospheric belt and hear the strange almost "elongated" sounds of full, vital space. He becomes a master of all things audible. He can hear a million notes, most of which he could not name. He could write, if he were consciously able to move that is, great symphonies of nature's wonderful sounds. He would speak, if he were capable of moving his lips, greater words than Shakespeare ever wrote.

The aspirant is now an adept.

If he can now, consciously, raise the power of *kundalini*, together with the forces of the throat centre, even higher so that the christ centre fully opens, he becomes a master for that time and he is capable of meditation for 5 minutes, 10 minutes, 50 years, 200 years; it does not matter. His body becomes completely immobile, almost cold. His breathing is barely perceptible. The only heat in the body is a thin band of warmth around the top of the forehead which stops rigor mortis from setting in and this warmth is just enough to keep the blood in a state of semi-suspension.

This is a metaphysical description of the true meditative state.

Cosmic Consciousness

There is an even higher state of consciousness than meditation, which has rarely been attained. Those who have fully entered this state are all masters of yoga and the mystic sciences. Sri Patanjali described it as seedless *samadhi* in that the final seed of the highest mental process (*samadhi*) has been transmuted and you have moved into a state of pure being. Nowadays it is known as cosmic consciousness.

In concentration you think about an object; in contemplation you tune into and receive the mind emanations contained in the object; in meditation you become one with the object; in cosmic consciousness you become one with that which is the object, and hence that which is all objects throughout the cosmos. Concentration is limited to the physical and mental aspect; contemplation includes the psychic aspect as well; meditation moves beyond this into the spiritual aspect. Cosmic consciousness is not limited to any aspect or even time frame; it includes them all; it is more even than a state of oneness—it can only be described as a state of being.

The following is a beautiful description of cosmic consciousness as experienced by Dr. King.

Deep breath. The tides of universal life force were drawn in, to be directed along the singing nerve sheaths by concentrated mind and thrown down hard to the base of the spine, there to be risen by mind, which knew only one objective—that of complete mastery over the latent powers within. Powers, which just awaited the key, the chord, to bring them into active, vibrant movement. Tremendous effort—and then "she", this great mysterious goddess—kundalini, which all men strive to raise, did move. This time though, apparently easier and even more surely than "she" had before. It was as though "she", in her grace, had decided that this was some divine and auspicious occasion.

Gently at first, creeping almost like a snake, "she" came upwards and ever upwards. The burning sensation in the base of the spine, which had been felt many times before, was experienced this time, but as if the Gods Themselves were standing guard over the adept. His detachment from the excruciating pain was even more complete than ever it had been before. "She" moved gently upwards and

when "she" pierced the solar plexus centre, even though his eyes were closed to the world, he could see more surely than ever he had when those eyes were physically opened.

He struggled on and gradually moved her through the solar plexus centre— climbing, creeping slowly, gently, yet as sure as the light of the sun, did he bring her upwards. Great rivers of perspiration streamed down his face and neck, even though he was so cold he could have wept. Though he could not move one leg, he shook as though afflicted with ague when his spine vibrated in sympathy with the tremendously powerful rising forces. When, after what seemed an age of shaking mental agony, in all her grace "she" dwelt within the heart centre, his vision was extended. No longer was the world built of gross physical matter, but had a strangely subtle pattern which normal man could not appreciate. No longer did a colour stand alone but was surrounded by musical tones which went resonating into the distance. Yet those ears could hear them, even to the farthest ends of this distance.

His vision was extended through the place he was in and beyond. It was as though he had all-seeing vision. Mysteries which had remained, to this day, like ancient charts lost beneath the ocean of forgetfulness, came before his eyes and he saw, read and understood them.

Then, steadfast, not content with even this, he fervently fought for her added grace to climb even further upwards.

And "she" came.

When "she" entered the throat centre, he sat immobile as one in physical death, yet pulsating with greater life than he had ever experienced before. As "she" entered and dwelt within the throat centre, "she" lent to this her grace and power and his world became one of sound as well as vision. A million sounds were appreciated. Those nerves within his body which were still alive, thrilled to the exotic, symphonic harmony of nature—itself. He felt, at that time, he was one with nature; but was soon to find that this was just a small beginning.

The great power rose upwards. As though by the grace of some invisible but merciful God, "she" rose, slowly, surely, creeping ever upwards, taking him into even higher realms than this. Then—all of a sudden, "she" emerged from the top of the spine and in a glorious flash, the christ centre was open. He began to know who he was and why he came. At this time, immobile, cold as if dead, he experienced even a greater life than most men have ever dreamed of and yet, in some strange way, was detached from it all. It was as though he, a light, was alone in the universe. It was as though he, at this moment, was being probed by a radiant beam of exploring intelligence, so intense, so ancient, so wise, that it knew his every movement from his initial birth a million, million years ago until this day—aye, and even beyond that, to some dim part of the future, so distant as to be beyond even his enhanced comprehension. The great light shone apparently through him to almost, what was to the adept, infinity, and seemed, in some strange way, to return to him with the wisdom of the ages collected by its immense journey.

As the great goddess of power dwelt within this chakra, the adept, in true deep meditation, became a knower. He felt that this state, despite his complete alone-ness, was the ultimate. He knew later that this feeling was but an expression of his ignorance, for suddenly, even as a great shock to him, this great power reached to the uppermost branch of the tree and then, gradually at first, but surely, the highest centre opened.

It was as though in a moment, he wore above his head a crown of indescribable magnificence!

A glorious brilliant flash of illumination came to him.

The powers before were nothing in comparison with this. Oh God, he was going even further upwards!

His loneliness subsided, as a calm will stop the turbulence of the waves at sea, and peace began—but not static peace, for in this was all movement. He began to stretch outward as though he had immense arms which were embracing all things. His consciousness reached out-ward—holding, and gradually came the realisation of oneness. No longer was he a light in the wilderness as he had been before, but now he was an essential part, an intimate part, an interrelated part of all things. His consciousness soared above the environment, above the city in which his cold body sat immobile, around the city, around all things and all people and all environment. Soaring upwards and out-ward, he was now in the full and complete realisation that he was life, which was manifesting in countless different ways in order to gain the experience necessary, the control demanded over matter itself. Here, in such an elevated state as this, came a deeper realisation than ever before of the interrelationship of all things, of the life of all things. When he dwelt for a moment upon a rock, it sprang into vibrant life before his "eye". It breathed, it had feeling, it had disappointment. The rock, in some vague way, experienced passion; it had a soul, a veritable spiritual essence which linked it with him, with all. As the state became even more advanced, he felt as though he was above the world, embracing it all, a part of it; living with it in complete intimacy; knowing it, appreciating it, loving it as he had never felt love before. He became one with that upon which his superconsciousness dwelt. He became detached from this oneness when he felt he should, in order to learn from the experience of detachment, and attached when he wanted to in order to learn from the experience of attachment.

He became existent in timelessness.

He became vitally aware of the dimensions in which he existed and knew them—aye, all seven of them. He became as tiny as a molecule when he wanted to and yet bigger than a world when he wished. He looked down from his lofty position high above the Earth, appreciating its great glory, its power, its supreme light; perceiving the limitations it had put upon itself in order to allow life streams like him to gain the very experience which he was now living through in almost godlike ecstasy. It was then, when this realisation dawned, that he stopped short.

Here was the very power which he had sought. Power beyond the wildest dreams, beyond the most imaginative conception of mere man; power to know what secrets he wished; power greater than that needed to move any mountain, anywhere, at any time. But yet, he stopped short, as though strangely disappointed with himself. Beneath him, beneath the crust of Earth, within the ancient globe, dwelt a greater being than he or all men. A being which had imposed upon itself, crushing limitations, so that the mass of men could crawl through existence upon its back in order to gain experience, knowledge and eventually—even wisdom.

It was as though he had learned the great lesson brought about by striving for this, what was to him then, an ultimate state of being. The lesson of detachment from even the greatest states he learned and gradually he came back, becoming smaller and smaller with every true spiritual desire. Gradually he crept away from his all-powerful state—slowly diminishing, until again he became the lonely light shining through space. He dimmed this as he brought the power of *kundalini* downward. As he descended the ladder from the lofty heights of cosmic consciousness, when *kundalini* passed through the throat centre, he became aware again of the world of sonic vibrations. He was tempted to linger here, but the haunting vision of that wonderful being, which was the Earth, suffering gross limitation to be the world, to be a sure home for crawling ignorant man who would be lost in space without her, caused him to leave the ecstasy of this sound plane, and downward came the *kundalini* until he became aware again of his coarse physical structure and of his gross limitations; of his cold shivering body and stiff aching limbs.

Dr. King demonstrates in this beautiful, technical description of the most elevated state of consciousness attainable on Earth, his true status as an advanced master in his own right. He also teaches us all a superb lesson by choosing to leave this state of ecstatic bliss when he realised, at the deepest possible level, the suffering of the Mother Earth and the need to give service in the light of her sacrifice.

Kundalini Yoga Breathing

A powerful series of exercises to achieve the higher states of consciousness

Dr. King considered very carefully before deciding to publish these exercises. They are the key to true samadhic meditation, but if they are not practised correctly, they can bring about a psychological imbalance. They are only for the advanced student who has decided to follow the path of spiritual development seriously. They should be practised in the context of a stable mental and emotional life, preferably with a balanced diet and regular exercise. They are based on the system of yoga breathing taught in the Fourth Initiation on pages 112-123, but instead of using the mental affirmations published with each of those exercises, you should use the following visualisations. These will cause the *kundalini* to rise upwards through the channel within the spine. You should have learned the six breathing exercises and the automatic counting method perfectly before using these advanced visualisations.

The First Breathing

The first breathing exercise is practised as follows: as you breathe in, visualise the *prana* entering the nose, then travelling over the top of the head, down each side of the spine to the base of the spine.

As you breathe out, visualise the *prana* travelling up the middle of the spine to the christ centre, which is situated between the eyebrows and a few inches in front of the forehead.

Practise this breathing until you feel ready to start the next exercise.

The Second Kundalini Yoga Breathing

A powerful series of exercises to achieve the higher states of consciousness

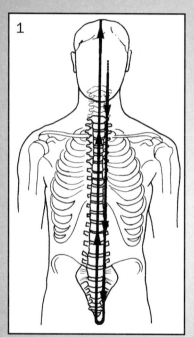

When you take the breath in, visualise *prana* coming in. If it is coming in through the left nostril [*] it will be a negative aspect of the universal life force. Think the *prana* in and request it to come in. Make a magnetic demand on the universal supply of energy that the air you breathe is vibrant with this great all-pervasive life force and pull it in through the left nostril and down the left side of the spine. When you feel that it gets to the bottom of the spine, attempt to think it into the spinal column during the time you hold the breath-into that tiny little channel, which is a hundredth part of a hair in breadth, existing within the spinal column. When you breathe out, visualise the *prana* travelling up *susumna* to the top of the head, out into the christ centre, and leave it there (see illustration 1). Then you do the same thing breathing through the right nostril, taking the *prana* down the right side of the spine, thinking it into the base of the spinal column while you hold the breath in, and then up *susumna* to the top of the head as you breathe out. (See illustration 2.)

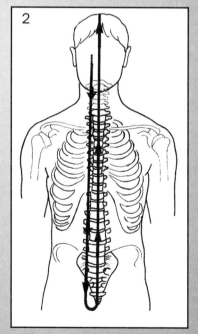

* You will note that in this exercise Dr. King has started with the left nostril rather than the right, as was taught on p.114. At this stage the student may decide whether it is more conducive to start with the left or right nostril.

The Third Kundalini Yoga Breathing

A powerful series of exercises to achieve the higher states of consciousness

You again take the breath in, say, through the left nostril and then out through the right. When you breathe it out through the right, visualise it coming up the channel in the spine to the head. When you hold the body empty of breath, try to transfer your consciousness to the christ centre. If you need an aid to visualisation, I suggest that you use a blue, equilateral triangle. Try to visualise this triangle as being as blue as a mid-summer sky, in front of the third eye. While you are visualising the blue triangle, curl your tongue back and touch the roof of your mouth with it gently. This will tend to stop the conscious mind from throwing up intervening thoughts which stop you from visualising the blue triangle. Correct pressure on the roof of the mouth with the tongue will inhibit the conscious mind from working for fractions of a second, allowing you to perform this wonderful concentration. Then you do the same thing breathing in through the right nostril, out of the left nostril and so on. This exercise will help you greatly to bring on meditation.

In the Second and Third Kundalini Breathings, when you feel ready to do so, you can extend the period of holding the breath, so that the rhythm changes from 1-2-1 to 1-3-1, 1-4-1 or 1-5-1.

The Fourth Kundalini Yoga Breathing

A powerful series of exercises to achieve the higher states of consciousness

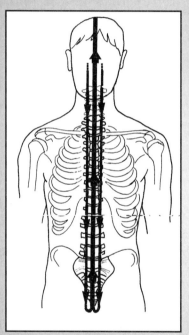

When you breathe in you make a request for *prana*. Draw it in with your mind. *Prana* is a magnetic energy and the brain is a magnet. If you use it correctly you can draw more *prana* in. When you draw the breath in, think the *prana* going right down the spine. Do not think it going down one side of the spine this time, but right down the spinal column. When you breathe out, think it coming up through the channel within the spinal column. You should do it quickly—the quicker you do it, the better it is. When you take the last breath and hold it in, visualise the *prana* as rising up through the psychic centres, and when you breathe out, think the *prana* as rising up the spine again to the christ centre (see illustration).

The Fifth and Sixth Kundalini Yoga Breathings

A powerful series of exercises to achieve the higher states of consciousness

The Fifth Breathing

This breathing is performed exactly as taught in the Fourth Initiation (page 120).

The Sixth Breathing

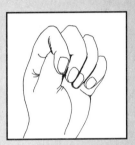

This exercise is performed as taught in the Fourth Initiation (page 122), except that as you breathe in you visualise *prana* as white light travelling up *susumna* from the base of the spine into the christ centre. After you have done the sixth exercise, put your hands on the knees, with the thumb clenched between the fingers of each hand (see illustration 7.4). Close your eyes and think the *kundalini* from the top of the spine downward. Let it come down through each psychic centre in turn and feel a great harmony and balance in the body. You can then say a prayer of thankfulness or chant a mantra. This brings an essential balance and control to the whole practice.

Controlling the Vital Life Fluid

According to the yogis, celibacy is an essential prerequisite to attaining enlightenment. This is not a moral teaching: it is a practical, scientific step which an individual can take if they choose. It is about controlling and transmuting sexual energy into something greater. It is not about suppression of sex impulses, which should certainly be avoided.

If the sex impulse is not controlled, two things happen. Firstly, you cannot raise the *kundalini* in its entirety above the sex centre, because the stimulation will be too great in that chakra. Secondly, the vital life fluid (termed as *ojas* in Sanskrit), which exists within the spinal column, will be dissipated and the highest states of consciousness cannot then be obtained. The following Tibetan exercise was taught by Dr. King for those advanced students who wish to control the vital life fluid.

When a sexual urge is felt, remain still, breathe through the nostrils, but imagine that the breath is entering the base of the spine. While breathing in, imagine the spine is gradually being filled like a cup until it reaches a point opposite the solar plexus centre.

Then, on breathing out, visualise the universal life force being pushed up the spine. We have certain glands in both man and woman that, when a sexual urge comes, become activated. The vital life fluid has leaked down from the brain. If you can bring it back up the spine you can put it back and fire the brain in a different way.

Then you can not only control—not suppress—this urge but also transmute it onto a much higher level. You can enhance your powers of concentration, contemplation and all your mystic abilities by doing this.

There are pearls in the deep sea, but one must hazard all to find them. If diving once does not bring you pearls, you need not therefore conclude that the sea is without them.

Dive again and again.

You are sure to be rewarded in the end.

Sri Ramakrishna

**Seize this very minute—
boldness has genius, power and magic in it.**

Johann Wolfgang von Goethe

Afterword

Until the 20th century there had never been a metaphysical concept of evolution beyond the state of cosmic consciousness. It was known in mystic circles that some who had entered this state, called *nirvana* in the east, could escape the wheel of rebirth and join the Great White Brotherhood (the Spiritual Hierarchy of Earth). They could then live for hundreds of years on Earth in the same physical body without aging, helping humanity in many unseen ways, the results of which have been indispensable. They had, in fact, been through the Initiation of Ascension, which the Master Jesus demonstrated so conclusively when he resurrected after the crucifixion.

But the process of evolution beyond this was not understood until two works were published: *The Twelve Blessings*, a beautiful and advanced system of white magic; and

The Nine Freedoms, which I regard as the greatest metaphysical treatise ever written. These two books by Dr. King trace a future beyond the western concept of heaven, the eastern concept of *nirvana*, and even the mystical Initiation of Ascension. Evolution continues on a myriad of planets, suns and galaxies in the cosmos, until we all return back to the Divine Source from which we came. This idea in itself was known and taught by the ancient rishis, but now a much fuller explanation has been given of what this really means.

The spiritual path includes hard work, sacrifice, discipline and tests, but even more than these things, it includes purpose, joy, accomplishment and ultimately, enlightenment itself. Life is not meant to be about suffering. By following the spiritual path laid down in this book you can avoid many needless, painful experiences and enjoy instead the incomparable feeling of true spiritual happiness. The yogis spoke often about bliss, ecstasy and deep inner peace. In these days of service it is sometimes necessary to turn away from these things in order to help others. But they will never be far from you if you include the spiritual practices Dr. King has revealed here. It is up to you how far and how fast you wish to realise your inner potential. Whatever your decision I recommend the following advice to you which was delivered by The Master Aetherius:

Be not sad, my friends, for you have nothing to be sad about.

Be joyful, be full of spiritual happiness and the fetters of your karma will fall from you.

Information from the publishers
Deeper into spiritual experience

This book has introduced many spiritual exercises designed to lead you through practice towards greater spiritual advancement and enlightenment. On this journey you will find yourself becoming strengthened and inspired by the new and exciting experiences you have. Such experiences are signposts on the road to your higher consciousness; they tell you that you are going in the right direction and show you that you are getting nearer and nearer to your goal.

Spiritual experience comes in many forms and from many sources, not just from practices which you perform in the quiet of your own room. Indeed, to put such practices to their highest use, the student must leave this quiet and take his or her new-found abilities out into the world and use them for the benefit of others. When we do, we begin to find ourselves having spiritual experiences of an entirely different order.

In this appendix we recommend three of the most powerful ways to do this. They are briefly mentioned as a guide to further practical study. Because of the constraints of space, they are only briefly explained. Much fuller information is available from the publishers upon request.

Spiritual experience comes in many forms and from many sources, not just from practices which you perform in the quiet of your own room.

Holy Mountains
– places of power

Spiritual students throughout the centuries have made pilgrimages to holy mountains, often with life-changing results. The seekers of the Far East traversed the snow-covered Himalayas seeking spiritual guidance; many peoples of the world have made vision quests to mountains and deserts seeking guidance from Mother Nature. It was known how important it was to leave the day-to-day surroundings of villages and towns, to be alone, open and centred, in order to hear the subtle messages from a higher source or from a higher part of oneself. In modern times it can be even more important.

The publishers strongly recommend the holy mountains listed below for such a pilgrimage. These mountains are special in that they have been charged with powerful energies by elevated spiritual beings. From such a charged place the pilgrim can send out tremendous healing power, for the world as whole or for an individual. When you do this and feel these powers flow through you, you will have one of the most uplifting experiences of your life. You will come away with a greater appreciation of the oneness of all life, and a realisation that service to others in this way can be a most glorious and inspiring thing.

Use the powerful practices given in this book in the surroundings of such a wonderful natural temple and you will rejoice that you chose to do so. We especially recommend that you use your visit for the practice of The Twelve Blessings.

The 19 mountains listed below range from climbs that are short, simple and safe, to ones which are arduous and hazardous. If you would like information on how to get to any of these mountains and what type of weather to expect, or if you would like to join with others on a pilgrimage led by experienced personnel, please contact The Aetherius Society.

British Isles and Europe

Holdstone Down, North Devonshire, England (nearest community: Combe Martin).

Yes Tor, South Devonshire, England (nearest community: Okehampton).

Brown Willy, Cornwall, England (nearest community: Bodmin).

Kinderscout, Derbyshire, England (nearest community: Hayfield).

Old Man, Coniston, Cumbria, England

(nearest community: Coniston).

Ben Hope, The Highlands, Scotland (nearest community: Tongue).

Creag-an-Leth-Chain, Grampian, Scotland (nearest community: Aviemore).

Carnedd Llywelyn, Gwynedd, North Wales (nearest community: Betws-Y-Coed).

Pen-Y-Fan, Powys, South Wales (nearest community: Brecon).

Mederger Flue, Swiss Alps, Switzerland (nearest community: Davos).

Le Nid D'Aigle, Mont Blanc, France (nearest community: Les Houches).

United States of America

Mount Baldy, San Antonio Mountain Range, Southern California (nearest community: Mount Baldy Village).

Mount Tallac, Sierra Nevada Mountain Range, Northern California (nearest community: Tahoe Valley).

Mount Adams, Presidential Range, New Hampshire (nearest community: Gorham).

Castle Peak, Rocky Mountains, Colorado (nearest community: Aspen).

Australia and New Zealand

Mount Kosciusko, Snowy Mountains, New South Wales, Australia (nearest community: Kosciusko National Park ski resort).

Mount Ramshead, Snowy Mountains, New South Wales, Australia (nearest community: Thredbo).

Mount Wakefield, Southern Alps, New Zealand (nearest community: The Hermitage, Mount Cook holiday resort).

Africa

Mount Kilimanjaro, Tanzania

One of a series of remarkable photographs of Dr. King on Mount Ramshead. Note the clearly visible energy field above him.

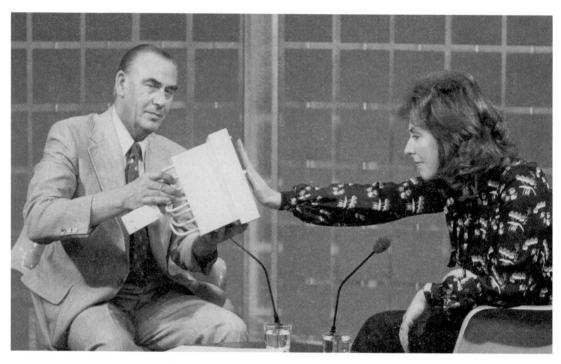

Dr. King with a model of his Spiritual Energy Battery showing how it is used in Operation Prayer Power

Operation Prayer Power
– spiritual energy meets technology

Operation Prayer Power was designed by Dr. King as a way for groups of people to use the techniques of prayer and mantra outlined in this book, as a powerful tool to help the world as a whole.

Through group participation at an Operation Prayer Power session, tremendous spiritual power can be invoked and, if you join in with the spirit of the occasion, you will really feel this spiritual energy coursing through you. Attenders join together for two hours in a powerful ritual that combines dynamic prayer, eastern mantra and mystic mudras.

What makes Operation Prayer Power unique is Dr. King's invention of a radionic battery which can actually store the energy which is invoked. As the sessions continue the battery becomes filled with energy resulting from thousands of man-hours of prayer.

Spiritual energy correctly used can have a significant effect on world conditions. Whenever there is a disaster which needs such energy, such as a hurricane, earthquake or war, Operation Prayer Power's store of uplifting healing energy can be released almost immediately through a radiation device in a fraction of the time it took to invoke. Such a concentration of prayer energy really does make a difference, sometimes in ways which seem almost miraculous.

The Aetherius Society has been performing Operation Prayer Power since 1973 and has had great success in helping victims of catastrophes and natural disasters.

Like the holy mountains, participating in Operation Prayer Power can be a wonderfully inspiring experience you will not forget. It is also a very beneficial manipulation of personal karma.

These sessions are open, in areas where it is held, to anyone who is willing to learn and practise the holy mantras used. Again, contact The Aetherius Society for further information.

Dr. King performs Tibetan Mudra Yoga to charge the Spiritual Energy Battery during an Operation Prayer Power charging session on Holdstone Down in North Devon, England.

Spiritual Pushes
– times of special power

If you believe in the possibility of more advanced life on other worlds, then you should investigate the Spiritual Pushes.

The Aetherius Society believes that, at specific times of the year, great power is made available to all spiritually-minded workers on Earth by certain highly evolved extraterrestrial Intelligences. At these times, anyone performing spiritual practices, or praying, or working in an unselfish manner (such as giving healing or working for world peace), will have those actions highly potentised. In this way, a concentration of spiritual power builds up on Earth and this affects all life for the better.

Again, if you go out of your way to cooperate with these Spiritual Pushes, you will have experiences that will surprise you and could change your life.

The Spiritual Push dates are the same each year, as follows:

April 18th to May 23rd

July 5th to August 5th

September 3rd to October 9th

November 4th to December 10th

They begin and end at 12 midnight Greenwich Mean Time at the end of the day in question.

Bibliography

Bailey, Alice A.
The Consciousness of the Atom
Lucis Publishing Co., 1922

Bedriji, Orest
You
Amity House Inc., 1988

Capra, Fritjof
The Tao of Physics
Wildwood House, 1975

King, D.D., Th.D., George
The Twelve Blessings, 1958
The Nine Freedoms, 1963
A Book of Sacred Prayers, 1966
You Too Can Heal, 1976
Karma and Reincarnation, 1986
Personal development cassette lectures

All books and tapes by Dr. George King are published by Aetherius Press.

Lao Tzu
Tao Te Ching
Penguin Books, 1963

Leadbeater, C.W.
The Science of the Sacraments
The Theosophical Publishing House, 1975

Prabhupada, His Divine Grace A.C. Bhaktivedanta Swami
Srimad Bhagavatam
Bhaktivedanta Book Trust, 1987

Ramacharaka, Yogi
The Science of Breath
 L.N. Fowler & Co., 1960

Rama Prasad, M.A.
Nature's Finer Forces
The Theosophical Publishing House, 1897

Sivananda, Swami
Mind - Its Mysteries and Control
Divine Life Society, 1946

Vivekananda, Swami
Raja Yoga
Advaita Ashrama, Himalayas, 1970

Wallis Budge, E.A.
The Book of the Dead
Arkana, 1989

Yogananda, Paramahansa
Autobiography of a Yogi
Rider & Co., 1950

Zukav, Gary
The Dancing Wu Li Masters
William Morrow & Co. Inc., 1979

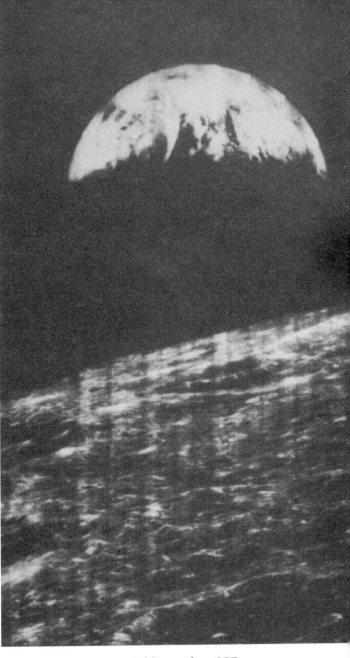

A wise man will make more opportunities than he finds.

Sir Francis Bacon

Index

Inner Potential Training

You can read *Realise Your Inner Potential* in a few hours, but you could spend a lifetime exploring the practices it contains.

London's Inner Potential Centre began in 1999, specifically to provide personal training on the techniques and practices taught in *Realise Your Inner Potential*. As well as workshops, courses and classes based on the book, the centre also presents ones that allow you to explore subjects such as healing, mantra, prayer, dowsing, psychic development and yoga breathing (to name just a few) in much greater depth and detail.

Inner Potential training is not confined to London. More centres are being established, and accredited instructors travel extensively to bring the wisdom of *Realise Your Inner Potential* to those who need it. You can come to us, or we will come to you.

For further information, visit:
www.innerpotential.org
email: info@innerpotential.org
or phone:

UK	**020 7736 4187**
USA	**1 800 800 1354**
New Zealand	**09 418 1170**

Bear in mind that Inner Potential training is growing all the time, so if you do not see your part of the world listed here, don't give up. Get in touch anyway—we may well be able to help you.

The topics covered in this book are also taught at Aetherius Society centres in Canada, Australia, Africa and Europe: www.aetherius.org.

May you find fun, adventure and fulfilment learning to **realise your inner potential**.